LATitude

LATitude

HOW TO MAKE A LIVE APART TOGETHER RELATIONSHIP WORK

VICKI LARSON

CLEiS
PRESS

Published in the United States by Cleis Press, an imprint of Start Midnight, LLC, 221 River Street, Ninth Floor, Hoboken, New Jersey 07030.

Printed in the United States
Cover design: Jennifer Do
Cover image: Shutterstock / Romolo Tavani
Text design: Frank Wiedemann

First Edition.
10 9 8 7 6 5 4 3 2 1

Trade paper ISBN: 978-1-62778-332-3
E-book ISBN: 978-1-62778-545-7

To my late mother,
Trude Janofsky, who made the bold move at
midlife to find a room of her own.

TABLE OF CONTENTS

INTRODUCTION:
THE ACCIDENTAL LAT

I'll be honest—for most of my life, the thought of living apart from my romantic partner just seemed stupid.

Why the heck would I want to live separately from the person I loved?

I didn't in my first marriage, a starter marriage of just a few years. In fact, I dropped out of college to follow him to Colorado because the thought of being halfway across the country from him seemed intolerable.

When I met the man who became my second husband, we were on opposite sides of the country, him in San Francisco and me in Miami. We lived apart for six months, flying back and forth monthly with lots of steamy phone calls and letters in between— this was before the Internet, email, and texting—until I landed a job in California forty-seven miles away from him. Obviously, we were not going to live together, and even when I rejected that job to take one that was a tad closer—forty miles away—I still planned to get my own place.

Except I struggled to find a place I could afford.

"Why don't you just move in with me?" he asked, and even though I wasn't prepared to live with someone I'd known only a few months, it sure beat paying twice as much for a cramped studio apartment above a bar that was about the size of the walk-in closet in my Miami condo.

Plus, I was madly in love with him. Living with the person you love is just something you do, no questions asked, right?

Like many people, I had an idea of what things were "supposed" to look like. I was aware of the romantic script many of us follow: meet, date, fall in love, wed, have kids, and live happily ever after—under the same roof, of course.

And that's what I did. Until it all came crashing down and I divorced again.

Newly single at age forty-eight and with two tween boys, I fell fast and hard for a man who also had a tween daughter. I didn't want to meld our families while his and my children were young, but I thought we'd eventually move in together. That old script of what a romantic relationship "should" look like is a hard one to bust. But whenever I brought it up, he was vague about living together, which at first made me feel bad and sad— didn't he love me?

Yet the longer we were together—committed, very much in love, and seeing each other a few times a week—the more I realized that this living-alone thing wasn't so bad. In fact, I began to like it. *A lot.*

So, for the first time in my life, I asked myself, What do I want my life to look like? Was it different from what I expected it "should" look like? At midlife, I already had much of what I wanted—two children, a house, a career—so I certainly didn't "need" a man.

I did, however, want a boyfriend. I just didn't want him hanging around all the time.

What I didn't even realize at the time was that I actually had a role model for how that could work—my mother. When she was in her forties, with both her daughters grown and out of the house, my mom left my dad and her comfortable suburban New York City home and moved to Miami, where my sister was living at the time. She bought a condo, got a job, and created a life for herself. It was the first time my mother, a Holocaust survivor who was orphaned in World War II and married my father a week before her twenty-first birthday, lived alone.

My parents didn't divorce, however—they had a live apart together (LAT) marriage. My father packed up our Yorkie, Teddy, and visited her for a long weekend every month. They did that for about ten years, until my father retired and joined her in Florida, where they lived together in somewhat peaceful coexistence until my mom died after sixty-one years of marriage.

When my mother made this bold decision, I wasn't really paying too much attention to what my parents were doing. But at midlife, divorced for the second time, and with two young children, I had a question for her: "What the heck, Mom?"

"I'd had enough," she told me. After two marriages and many years as a wife and mother, I knew *exactly* what she meant.

Many older women like my mom and me have come to realize that living apart from a romantic partner allows us to have the best of both worlds—companionship as well as independence. It also frees us from the gendered caretaking and housekeeping women often do. According to a 2011 study, many older single women would like to have a companion but were adamant that they were "willing to be lonely before sacrificing independence."[1]

Which is perhaps why the growing live apart together lifestyle choice is overwhelmingly driven by women.

In a survey of close to five hundred people that my co-author and I conducted for our 2014 book, *The New I Do: Reshaping Marriage for Skeptics, Realists and Rebels*, nearly seventy-five percent of the respondents said they wanted a marriage that "allows independence." What better way to maintain independence than as live apart together partners?

In fact, live apart together relationships have been called the "gender revolution continuing into old age,"[2] according to Swedish researchers Sofie Ghazanfareeon Karlsson and Klas Borell—a nod to the fact that baby boomer women have been on the forefront of restructuring family life in the past few decades, especially after no-fault divorce was written into law across the United States.

As much as many heterosexual women desire equality in their marriages, the truth is many do not achieve it. I finally did, but only after I divorced, when my former husband and I had fifty-fifty physical custody of our boys, one week with me, one week with him. Having time to myself not only rejuvenated me but it made me a better mother, friend, journalist, and romantic partner. It gave me much-needed self-care and space.

Is divorce the only way a couple can have more equality in their relationship and me time? No. Could they have that if they stayed together?

Yes, as live apart together partners.

It isn't just older heterosexual women who find living apart from their romantic partner a plus, however. Many same-sex couples, especially gay men, do, too. Some parents have young children from previous marriages or relationships, as I did, and either don't want to move them away from the family house and neighborhoods, schools, and friends, or can't move to be closer to a new romantic partner because they share custody. Those who embrace polyamory, solo polyamory (when someone has multiple intimate relationships but prefers an independent lifestyle), and ethical nonmonogamy are also often drawn to living apart. Other couples choose to live apart because they've hit a rough patch in their marriage and need space but don't want to divorce—like my mom. Many romantic partners say living apart has brought them closer.

Not to say that couples can't get closer while living under the same roof, but here's something that often happens when couples live together—they begin to take their partner for granted. Life is busy, they're distracted, they want things to be easy or at least less stressful, and so they go into roommate mode, occupying the same space but not necessarily engaging in meaningful, intimate ways. You can easily forget to appreciate, or even notice, the small things your partner does to make your life enjoyable, and they may also miss your good intentions. That complacency can lead to living life side by side without enjoying all the aspects of the relationship, and your partner, that drew you to each other in the first place.

Just because you're living together doesn't mean that you are always connecting with each other in significant ways. In fact, people spend hours a day on their smartphones, tablets, and streaming.[3] There is little that's intimacy-building or meaningful about that (unless streaming a series about someone else's hard times or dysfunctional marriage helps you appreciate your own relationship better, and there's some research to indicate that may be so).[4]

That hasn't happened with me and any of my partners, or any of the live apart together couples I spoke to for this book. If anything, research shows that couples who live apart from each other work harder at staying connected. You have to plan the times you're going to be together, and then when you are together, you're much more engaged and in the moment—not just occupying the same space.

Speaking of intimacy, here's one of the best perks of living apart from your partner—more sex and more satisfying sex. Given that so many people say they are in sexless marriages, living apart just may be the key to keeping desire alive. In fact, studies indicate that women who don't live with their partners retain their desire much more than women who do.

"Home, marriage, and motherhood have forever been the pursuit of many women," famed psychotherapist Esther Perel writes, "but also the place where women cease to feel like women."[5] And according to a recent study, unmarried couples who live apart report the highest levels of sexual satisfaction. And who doesn't want that (assuming you're interested in sex, that is)?

Actor Gillian Anderson understands the attraction of the live apart together lifestyle. As she says about her romantic partner, producer Peter Morgan, "My partner and I don't live together. If we did, that would be the end of us. It works so well as it is—it feels so special when we do come together."[6]

So does Helen Fisher, the biological anthropologist, best-selling author, and adviser to the Internet dating site Match.com. She and her husband, the *New York Times* columnist John Tierney, whom she married in 2020 when she was seventy-five and he was sixty-seven, don't live together. Instead, she has her place in Manhattan and he has his in the Bronx, and they spend a few nights together and a few apart each week. "I miss him terribly," she admits, "but it's a great way to have a really long-term romance."[7]

Plus, when they don't see each other every day, couples find new ways to create intimacy—it isn't just about touch and inter-course, which sometimes becomes problematic as we age and isn't always an option for some people with disabilities.

Clearly, in some cases, absence really does make the heart grow fonder.

What that absence looks like depends on the couple. It could be separate bedrooms in the same house, often unfortunately called a "sleep divorce"; two apartments in the same building; two condos in different cities; or two houses a few states—or countries—away from each other. Each live apart together arrangement is unique to the couple and mutually agreed upon to suit each partner's needs. Which, of course, brings up some obvious questions: "Shouldn't spouses put aside their own needs (and freedom) for the betterment of the couple?" "Isn't that one of the fundamental reasons for getting married—because two people want to spend their lives together and bring out the best in each other while celebrating togetherness?" "Where is the togetherness when you're living apart? Isn't it selfish?"

Those are important questions. However, togetherness doesn't always lead to more intimacy and warm and fuzzy feelings about your partner. Too much togetherness, as we've seen during the COVID-19 pandemic, can lead to arguments, anger, frustration, resentment, and perhaps even an ugly uncoupling.

While it's hard to get a good handle on just how many people live apart from their romantic partners, it's estimated that some ten percent of adults in Western Europe, the United States, Canada, New Zealand, and Australia don't live with their romantic partner.[8] In Britain alone, nearly a quarter of people statistically defined as "single" actually have a romantic partner who lives elsewhere.[9]

Regardless of how many live apart together couples exist now, social scientists are keenly aware that the phenomenon is growing. And for good reason. Living apart together can offer commitment, love, intimacy, stability, equality, sex, and all the other things many of us want in a romantic relationship while still giving us that much-desired but elusive room of our own. There aren't many types of romantic arrangements that can offer that. In fact, I can't think of any besides a live apart together arrangement.

Living apart together is hardly a new concept, but it's one that seemingly is a good fit for how we live and love in the twenty-first century. We are seeing huge shifts in our romantic landscape. Fewer young people are getting married, and the ones who are tying the knot are increasingly marrying later. More people are marrying multiple times, while others are happily choosing to remain single. People are having fewer children, many are choosing to be childfree, and some are becoming single parents by choice. And the world is rapidly aging, and many people, especially the divorced or widowed, who are no longer raising children may not want to uproot themselves to share a home with a new romantic partner somewhere far away from family and community. The "traditional" nuclear family (a married father and mother and their children all residing in one household), which is a relatively recent concept, is no longer the dominant family form.

Finally, we have numerous options on how to be partnered or not.

Still, despite the growing numbers of couples who live apart, few people discuss the topic openly, making it one of the last great taboos in love and sex. Many who choose this way of living and loving feel stigmatized, invalidated, misunderstood, and invisible.

In 2015 Sharon Hyman, a Montreal filmmaker, started a private Facebook page cleverly named "Apartners" for people who live apart from their romantic partner, as she has for more than two decades. Almost all the people asking to be a member said the same thing: "I thought we were the only ones. I'm so happy to know we're not."

Which is why I decided to write this book.

To be clear, I am not saying that living apart from your romantic partner is better than living together, although it may turn out that way for some couples. I am not advocating for couples living apart. What I am advocating for is letting people know that they have options in how they would like to arrange their romantic life, including living apart together.

Throughout this book, I will often abbreviate "live apart together relationships" to LAT and say "LAT couples" to refer to two people in a live apart together relationship. I will also sometimes call people LATs, acknowledging that some people who embrace the lifestyle are polyamorous or solo polyamorous and thus more than a couple. They are sometimes married and sometimes not. They are sometimes heterosexual and sometimes queer. I use actual names when they are referenced as such in published articles and online, and when I have gotten permission from those I've quoted and interviewed. I use pseudonyms when requested by those I've interviewed and who gave me permission to share their stories.

Chapter 1 asks and answers the first question many people are curious about—why live apart? In Chapter 2, we'll explore who's doing it and why, including the history of the trailblazing queer community and cultures over time and throughout the world, as well as present-day LATs. Chapter 3 is all about busting the myths of living apart together (for example, that you have to be wealthy, because you don't), while Chapter 4 walks you through how and when to start the conversation with a potential or new partner, how and when to start the conversation with a current partner, how and when to tell families and friends, and how to handle the people who just don't get it as well as your own ambivalence about it. I'll address the practicalities of making LAT relationships work in Chapter 5—how often, how far, whose house—the financial realities in Chapter 6, and the legal issues in Chapter 7. Chapter 8 dives into the experiences and challenges of living apart together with minor children, while Chapter 9 is all about sex and intimacy. Chapter 10 tackles aging apart, including retirement, caregiving, adult children, and end-of-life concerns. Chapter 11 details how some couples have decided to live apart to save their marriage. Finally, I look at the future of LAT as a family form, and how it could transform society for the better, in Chapter 12.

In every chapter, you'll discover the pros and cons of living apart together directly from people who have chosen this lifestyle as well as from research and experts. You may be surprised by how many studies note the numerous benefits a LAT relationship offers.

And hopefully, by the end of this book, you'll have a much clearer picture of whether living apart from your romantic partner is right for you.

"Knowing how to be solitary is central to the art of loving. When we can be alone, we can be with others without using them as a means of escape," the late poet and academic bell hooks wrote.[10]

1 | WHY LIVE APART?

Here's a question we rarely if ever hear—why do romantic partners live together?

It's just what couples *do*, right?

But why? Whose idea was it to insist that couples live together?

There's no way to know of course, although marriage historian and Evergreen State College professor emerita Stephanie Coontz tells me that throughout most of history, households were not just about raising children but also the center of production, so anyone who worked needed to be in one place. She also notes, "It took a certain amount of capital to set up a household, so people often didn't marry until they could do so, and people who could not afford to set up a little family farm or business worked as servants or lived as household dependents in the homes of those who could, even if they were married to someone who worked and lived in another household."[11]

We no longer live like that, of course. That said, we can all agree that before two people become a romantic couple, they start off as LATs, with each of them having a place of their own, whether solo or with parents, friends, roommates, or some other configuration. In other words, all romantic couples start off living in separate households.

And throughout history and even until today in parts of the world, some romantic couples stay that way.

First, let's look at married couples, because for many years, society looked down upon people of opposite sexes living together "in sin," although many US states recognized common-law marriages in the nineteenth and early twentieth centuries. That changed by the mid-twentieth century, when, after much debate in the courts, it lost its legal status.[12]

It wasn't until the late twentieth century that cohabitation became more acceptable and even trendy.[13]

In his 1949 book, *Social Structure*, anthropologist George Peter Murdock defined marriage as "a social group characterized by common residence, economic cooperation, and reproduction."[14] But as Coontz notes in her book *Marriage: A History*, sharing a residence is not universal for many couples, married or not. Both the Ashanti men of Ghana and Indonesia's Minangkabau men live with their mothers and sisters even after they wed. The men of New Guinea's Gururumba people sleep in separate housing, only coming together to cook and eat the day's main meal. And in eighteenth-century Austria, lower-class married couples often lived apart for years, mostly because they were servants living in other people's houses.[15]

The Mosuo people of southwest China have been extensively written about for practicing what's called a walking marriage, although they traditionally haven't married. Mosuo men visit their female lovers at night at their places and go back to their mothers' houses in the morning to help raise their sisters' children and grandchildren and contribute to the daily chores of their own extended family. That means instead of living with their parents under one roof, Mosuo children live with their mother in her multigenerational house, a model for LAT couples with young children that we'll discuss in more detail in Chapter 8.

There were no problems with this arrangement until the Chinese government instituted its "One Husband, One Wife" campaign in 1975, forcing the Mosuo to build houses so married couples could live together under one roof. This did not go over well, as sociologist Judith Stacey details in her 2012 book, *Unhitched: Love, Marriage, and Family Values from West Hollywood to Western China*. In fact, it caused huge disruptions.

"Mosuo adults who lived through the marriage campaigns recount endless stories of domestic disharmony and even violence unleashed by this coerced cohabitation, especially when women were forced to move in with their husbands' families or to live with their husbands and children in modern nuclear households," she writes.[16]

In 1981, the Mosuo were allowed to return to their traditional customs, which they did happily.

It's likely that walking marriages wouldn't be all that popular in the Western world, yet the US has a history of keeping spouses apart. For nearly 250 years, African Americans were beholden to their white slaveholders, who often determined which couples could marry and which had to separate. Rather than agree to the typical "until death do us part" wedding vows, African Americans couples instead had to answer, "Do you take this woman or this man to be your spouse—until death *or distance* do you part?"[17]

The US federal government also forced husbands and wives to separate when they created laws to break up the plural marriages of Native American tribes, Mormons, and immigrants in the 1800s. Still, each man was allowed to keep one wife.[18]

But if anyone did the most to keep husbands and wives apart, it probably was the Victorians.

Since as far back as we can go in human history, people slept together. Spouses, children, servants, strangers, friends, mistresses—whomever. Communal sleeping made sense, not only for safety but for warmth. [19]

Enter the Victorians with their prudish and virtuous attitudes, and communal sleeping seemed more than just improper—it was considered immoral. It started with the upper class, who had the space and money to give every family member their own bedroom, including husbands and wives, but it eventually caught on with the lower classes.

Having a "room of one's own," or at least a bed of one's own, was particularly popular with wives.

A "new woman" was emerging in the nineteenth century, *Atlas Obscura* observes. "She no longer wanted to be subservient to her husband and she actively claimed a new level of autonomy within her marriage. This shift was displayed in the middle-class bedroom where sexual boundaries were redrawn once again. In the grand old debauched marriage bed, wives were always available to their husbands. Separate beds marked an equipoise between the couple."[19]

After World War II, however, when there was a push for family togetherness, sleeping in separate beds was seen as indicating a troubled, loveless, and sexless marriage, a myth that persists today, writes certified behavioral sleep medicine specialist Wendy M. Troxel.[20] By the late 1970s, most spouses had gone back to sleeping together in a marital bed, and sleeping separately was seen as odd.

Since the 1990s, there has been a rise in unmarried couples who move in together. Their reasons are not unexpected—love and companionship, according to a 2019 Pew Research Center survey. That said, about four in ten couples say they decided to live with their romantic partner because it made financial sense or because it was convenient.[21]

Convenience is not the best reason to move in with your romantic partner. And we should ask: Convenient for *whom*?

Living together tends to be a heavier burden for women in heterosexual relationships than for men. As Maria Brandén and Karen Haandrikman discovered in their research, women are more likely to uproot their lives and move for the sake of living with their male romantic partners than vice versa. And if anyone's career prompts a long-distance move, it's typically his over hers—"nearly completely explained by power imbalances in the couple," they observe—and her career will more likely suffer because of it.[22]

And if she doesn't move closer?

What sociologist Sandra Krapf found is that couples who have to travel more than an hour to see each other are more likely to break up than those who live closer to each other. At the same time, she observes, those who live closer to each other are more likely to move in together than those in long-distance relationships.[23]

There's also a problem with couples who move in together because of financial reasons. You're basically turning a romantic decision—"I love my partner and I want to live with them and all their peccadilloes 24-7"—into a financial decision: "It sure would be cheaper if we lived together."

And yes, it would be cheaper. Living together under one roof and pooling resources usually boosts the economic situation of each person—one mortgage or rental payment; one utility bill;

one set of dishes, pots and pans, and flatware. Keeping two separate households often, but not always, is more expensive than cohabiting.

Yet looking solely at the financial savings of moving in together doesn't take into consideration other costs, such as the psychological cost if you have to live farther away from your own social network of family and friends. As Eli J. Finkel notes in his 2017 book, *The All-or-Nothing Marriage: How the Best Marriages Work*, expecting our romantic partner to be our everything—best friend, passionate lover, devoted coparent, soul mate, and great communicator, as well as our romantic, intellectual, and professional equal who provides us with happiness, financial stability, intimacy, and social status—is too much for any one person to fulfill. Finkel, a professor of psychology at Northwestern University and director of the Relationships and Motivation Lab, advocates for having "other significant others" (OSO)—family, neighbors, or friends who help us meet our needs (and hopefully vice versa).[24] You can see how problematic it may be if you have to move away from your OSO.

Also, if each partner has their own housing, one might be larger, or more valuable, or in a more desirable location, which could also complicate the transition from LAT to cohabitation.

"If you have two separate homes, you have twice the expenses, but there are cost benefits to everything," Debra A. Neiman, a certified financial planner and principal of Neiman & Associates Financial Services, tells me. "There're two lenses, a financial lens and an emotional lens. Minimizing the [financial] cost may not always be the best thing for the couple emotionally."[25]

WHAT DOES LAT MEAN?

The term "live apart together" didn't enter our consciousness until Irene Levin, of Oslo Metropolitan University in Norway, and Jan Trost, of Sweden's Uppsala University, coined the term in 1999.[26]

But it was Dutch journalist Michel Berkiel who first deemed the lifestyle "LAT," Levin observes, rejecting the term "living apart together" as being "too long" for an article he wrote about it—and the living arrangement he himself enjoyed—in the *Haagse Post* in 1978. LAT/lat was already a word in the Dutch language (it means "stick," which sounds promising for a romantic relationship you'd like to last), which, she says, "made its usage easier to accept." Now LAT is integrated into everyday speech in the Netherlands, she observes, although the concept has other names in other countries—*særbo* in Norway, *särbo* in Sweden, *cohabitation intermittente* in France, *partnerschaften mit getrennten haushalten* in Germany, and *liang tou hun*, or two-sided marriage, in China.

To be considered a LAT, three things must happen, according to Levin: the couple agrees that they are indeed a committed romantic couple, others view them as a committed romantic couple, and they must live in separate places. [27]

Levin considers it a new family form. "To be a couple is no longer dependent upon sharing a common household. It is no longer important for one to be married or to be living in the same household—one can still be a couple, and it is that to which the new term, LAT relationship, refers," Levin writes.[27]

While that covers many LAT couples, it doesn't cover all of them, and so to make this book as inclusive as possible, I am including LAT couples who live on different levels or different parts of the same household or have different bedrooms in the same household. I am also including people who are polyamorous and may have more than one partner, including solo polyamorists (someone who participates in multiple intimate relationships, but prefers an independent or single lifestyle).

I am not including people who are in long-distance relationships or commuter relationships, however. Those relationships are often more about some sort of constraint such as work or education and typically are not a choice of how they'd truly like to structure their romantic life. And living together at some point is often the end goal. I am also not including the millions of people who leave their homes to work abroad to provide better lives for their families. People who choose to be LATs are making a conscious decision because it generally suits their needs as individuals and as partners.

As you can see, defining a LAT relationship isn't all that easy, and because researchers often approach it from various viewpoints, the results of their studies aren't always comparable, notes Karen Upton-Davis, assistant professor in the School of Population Health, Discipline of Social Work, and Social Policy at the University of Western Australia, in Perth.[28] That said, because it is a growing phenomenon with societal implications, the Task Force on Families and Households came up with a definition in 2009 that would apply to the fifty-six countries within the United Nations Statistical Commission and Economic Commission for Europe (UNECE). Employing some of the language used by John Clifford Haskey, an associate fellow in the Department of Social Policy and Intervention at Oxford University who has extensively researched live apart together relationships in the United Kingdom, defines it as "a relationship, which is understood to include a romantic relationship, between partners who have their own separate address. That is, they usually live at different addresses to each other but they regard themselves as a couple and are recognized as such by others."

However, the task force also recognizes that while not sharing a common household is one of the fundamental tenets of a LAT relationship, "this concept may be difficult to measure in practice because it could be based on a variety of indicators." So, it suggests instead that "a subjective interpretation on the part of respondents whether or not they maintain separate households, i.e., live apart, with a LAT partner may offer the most feasible approach to measuring this living arrangement," which is more aligned with the definition of LAT I am using in this book.[29]

So, the big question is, "Why live apart from your romantic partner?" People have lots of different reasons to choose this arrangement, which we'll explore in Chapter 3, that probably have nothing to do with what years of research on the lifestyle say. Most of us don't turn to studies to determine how to structure our relationships, romantic or not. That said, there are a lot of studies that indicate that live apart together relationships offer as much good stuff as live-in relationships and, perhaps surprisingly, sometimes even more.

Before we delve into the research, however, consider what famed Belgian psychotherapist and author Esther Perel writes in her 2006 book, *Mating in Captivity: Unlocking Erotic Intelligence*. Love longs for closeness, she says, but desire thrives on distance.

"Our need for togetherness exists alongside our need for separateness. One does not exist without the other. With too much distance, there can be no connection. But too much merging eradicates the separateness of two distinct individuals. Then there is nothing more to transcend, no bridge to walk on, no one to visit on the other side, no other internal world to enter. When people become fused—when two become one—connection can no longer happen. There is no one to connect with. Thus separateness is a precondition for connection: this is the essential paradox of intimacy and sex."[30]

As I wrote in the introduction, I can't think of any romantic arrangement that can offer connection and separateness besides a live apart together relationship.

Luckily, research has my back.

THE GOOD STUFF

When I wrote the chapter on LAT relationships in *The New I Do*, I listed all the good aspects about them, based on interviews with LAT couples and studies:[31]

- LATs have the same or even higher levels of stability than couples who live together.
- LAT couples are as satisfied or more satisfied with their relationships than couples who live together.
- LAT couples have the same or even higher levels of commitment than couples who live together.
- LATs feel the same amount of trust or more trust for their partner than couples who live together.
- A LAT relationship offers a healthy balance between personal fulfillment and intimacy.
- Living apart often means couples don't focus on the negative and trivial behaviors—like uncapped toothpaste tubes or piles of papers, etc.—that can sometimes frustrate partners.
- Couples who live apart don't have the same constraints that living together entails, so it's easy for them to feel more confident that they are in the relationship for the right reasons.
- LATs don't feel claustrophobic.
- There may be less conflict.

- Each person is freer to pursue their own goals, passions, activities, friendships, and hobbies without having to check in with the other partner.

- Each person can focus on their career.

- Each person is less likely to feel like they've given up something for their partner.

- Couples are less likely to feel that they don't have a separate identity from their partner.

- Time spent together is often much more romantic and passionate.

- Sex can be more exciting.

- Relationships, especially marriages, tend to be more egalitarian.

- There's a sense that each partner is willing to sacrifice for the other's benefit.

- If one or both have children from previous relationships, they don't have the stress over the complications of combining families.

- It gives couples space to closely reexamine their relationship and find other ways to understand their partner.

- In certain situations, it may give couples time to think things through before responding.

- It helps people better cope with whatever insecurities come with romantic relationships.

- If the relationship ends, each person still has a place to live, removing that stress, and they may handle the breakup better.

Before we get into the research behind all that, it's important to acknowledge that having a romantic relationship is not *all that* for many people, such as aromantics, a term people who experience no romantic attraction use to define themselves, according to AUREA (Aromantic-spectrum Union for Recognition, Education, and Advocacy), an online initiative that seeks to further recognition and education around aromantics.[32]

In addition, there are some people who identify as relationship anarchists, a term coined by Swedish activist Andie Nordgren for people who don't privilege their romantic/sexual relationships over other types of relationships, typically platonic.

As Nordgren writes in her manifesto on making relationship anarchy work, "Life would not have much structure or meaning without joining together with other people to achieve things— constructing a life together, raising children, owning a house or growing together through thick and thin. Such endeavors usually need lots of trust and commitment between people to work. Relationship anarchy is not about never committing to anything—it's about designing your own commitments with the people around you, and freeing them from norms dictating that certain types of commitments are a requirement for love to be real, or that some commitments like raising children or moving in together have to be driven by certain kinds of feelings."[33]

Still, we live in a world that wants to thrust romantic partnerships upon everyone, what philosopher Elizabeth Brake calls "amatonormativity"—the belief that everyone desires an exclusive, long-term, coupled romantic relationship.[34] I'm going to assume (dangerous, I know) that since you picked up this book, you are interested in romantic relationships or are already in one (or several) or might be interested in one if you could create one that gave you the best of both single life and partnered life, a seemingly impossible task.

CLOSE, BUT NOT TOO CLOSE

Numerous studies point to the importance of close relationships, whether with family or friends or both, and even what sociologist Mark Granovetter calls "weak-tie" relationships, like the ones we have with the barista at a local coffee shop who knows us by name and exactly how we like our latte, the bus driver who is behind the wheel of the six forty-five a.m. express bus, or the hairstylist who makes us look our best no matter what we ask them to do. [35]

Society tends to privilege romantic relationships over platonic ones, and much has been written challenging that. Still, since romantic partnerships are viewed as the closest type of relationship an adult can have, lots of studies have explored what leads to long-term relationship satisfaction.

What they've found is that the quality and stability of a couple's relationship depend a lot on the amount of closeness they experience.

And therein lies the rub.

As we saw during the coronavirus pandemic, when many couples who typically would be out of the house because of work or other activities suddenly found that they couldn't spend much if any time apart, being together 24–7 led to more annoyance and arguing between partners.[36]

Too much closeness can negatively impact the relationship as well as each person's well-being. As much as we may want to be close to our romantic partner, we also have agentic needs, meaning our sense of freedom, independence, and self-mastery. If that closeness interferes too much with our agentic needs, well, it's troubling for the relationship.

Given that, how do we find a path forward if we want to honor ourselves as well as our romantic partner or partners? One study looked at romantic couples who live together and those who live apart. Their findings? "Although, on average, high objective closeness is experienced as positive, this beneficial effect is diminished or even reversed if the partners hold strong agency motives. . . . One plausible strategy to avoid such negative outcomes is the choice of LAT as a permanent living arrangement."[37]

While I personally believe that to be true, I wasn't the one to say it. But I'm sure happy someone did.

It really doesn't matter how physically close you are to your partner as long as each of you feels as close as you want to be, even if it isn't close by other people's desires, says David M. Frost, a psychologist and professor of population and family health at the Mailman School at Columbia University. His research finds that if someone feels "too close" or "not close enough" to their partner, they were more likely to become dissatisfied with their relationship, often leading to a breakup.[38]

Closeness is, of course, something romantic partners want from their relationship. Couples are expected to spend a lot of time together and do things together, not only as a twosome, but also with friends (often other couples) and family. Being part of each other's families and meeting and hanging out with each other's friends is part of the couple narrative,[39] even if you don't particularly care for your partner's friends or family. That can cause rifts between couples. Having a place of your own helps to create boundaries that allow each partner to decide whom to integrate into their relationship and whom to exclude, as well as when and how often. This seems to work well for women past the age of fifty in new relationships who are particularly interested in guarding their time with their children or grandchildren.[40]

As Levin observes, divorced or widowed people who seek a LAT arrangement see their new romantic relationship as an addition to the relationships they already have, not as something "instead."[27]

In Laura Stafford's 2004 book, *Maintaining Long-Distance*

and Cross-Residential Relationships, the professor of interpersonal communication at Bowling Green State University found that couples who live apart from each other not only feel as stable, satisfied, committed, and trusting as couples who live together, but they often have even higher levels of stability, satisfaction, commitment, and trust. In short, they have to work harder at their relationship.

While few if any of us enter into a romantic relationship hoping it will end, most of us understand on a certain level that it will, either by death or the other reason—one or both of you wants it to end. While some couples are able to stay in one household together after a breakup—and as more couples "consciously uncouple" and seek kinder, gentler partings, especially if they have minor children still at home—most of us do not. If you've always had your own place, however, the shock value is less.[41]

This is particularly important for divorced women. One study of baby boomer women found that leaving the home they lived in with their former spouse and perhaps raised children in after a divorce "played a large role in forming their identity, and for those people it was difficult to dissolve or leave the home."[42]

Divorce and separation also negatively impact one's residential and housing conditions in ways that may last for years, note Julia Mikolai, Hill Kulu, and Clara H. Mulder in the introduction to the special collection on "Separation, Divorce, and Residential Mobility in a Comparative Perspective," often to smaller, lower-quality rental units and out of homeownership. Women, they write, "are generally worse off than men and the negative effects are pronounced for individuals with low socioeconomic status."[43]

Divorce is hard enough; having a place of your own throughout your romantic relationship helps to alleviate some of that difficulty.

CHANGING WOMEN'S LIVES

Research has found that live apart together arrangements uniquely benefit (presumably heterosexual) women in many ways—sorry, guys! In their study of how living arrangements impact health, Harriet Young and Emily Grundy, of the London School of Hygiene and Tropical Medicine, found that in England, women in their sixties and older rated their health better if they lived alone instead of with a husband.[44]

In addition, for many heterosexual women, living separately from their romantic partner is a way to avoid unequal gender divisions of household labor and hands-on caregiving—"what can be seen as an obligation imposed by society"—as well as any troubling or controlling male behavior, observes Upton-Davis.[28]

This is particularly true in Japan, where marriage follows strict gendered roles that have the wife "playing the role of maid or mother while their husbands dedicate themselves to work." Many wives fear that expectation will get worse once their husband retires. So many older women embrace *sotsukon*, a combination of the Japanese words for "graduation" and "marriage" that describes an older married couple who stay legally married but live apart or share the same house but live independently from each other, also known as *kateinai bekkyo*, according to Japanese writer Yumiko Sugiyama, who explores the concept in her 2004 book, *Sotsukon no Susume (Recommending the Graduation from Marriage)*. Perhaps not surprisingly, the concept is viewed more favorably by women than men.[45]

Finally, more wives than husbands say they just don't have enough space to themselves, according to Terri Orbuch, a psychologist, author, and research professor at the University of Michigan's Institute for Social Research who has been following 373 married couples for more than three decades.[46] That's partly because women tend to do more of the caregiving for children or aging parents, or both, even if they also work outside the house.[47] Wives as well as husbands told Orbuch that the lack of privacy and time to focus on themselves was why they were unhappy in their marriage—almost twice as many as those who told her they were unhappy with their sex lives.

All of which leads Upton-Davis to conclude that "LAT has the potential to change women's lives for the better."[48]

That said, the idea of women preferring a LAT relationship to "undo gender" has been challenged by Simon Duncan, an emeritus professor in social policy at the University of Bradford who has written numerous papers on LATs. Hold that thought: we'll discuss his findings later in this chapter, when we explore the downsides of LAT relationships (yes, there are some).

There are several studies indicating that living apart from your romantic partner benefits your sex life. This may seem counterintuitive—wouldn't having your lover in bed next to you, or at least in the same room, lead to more sex because you've both available? Except, just sharing a bed or a bedroom doesn't automatically lead to more sex.

In her 2013 article "Living Apart, Together: Why Some Couples are Forgoing Cohabitation," social psychologist Samantha Joel, an assistant professor at Western University in Canada, acknowledges that while there is no research on how LAT relationships may help prevent a relationship from becoming monotonous per se, there are studies on long-distance relationships that can shed light on how living apart may create much-needed novelty and excitement. Citing numerous studies, she notes that couples who live far from each other "tend to experience more passion in their relationships than couples in geographically close relationships . . . idealize their partners more, meaning that they see their partners in unrealistically positive terms (which is generally a good thing) . . . spend more time reminiscing or daydreaming about their relationships, and they report more romantic love for their partners."[49]

And here's a surprising finding—the *less* face time the couples have, the stronger those effects are.

Part of the problem is that women who've been with their male romantic partner for between one and four years tend to lose their desire for him, according to Dietrich Klusmann, a psychologist at the University of Hamburg–Eppendorf in Germany, who has studied the bedroom habits of longtime couples.[50] Another British study of heterosexual and homosexual couples also found women who had been with their partner for more than five years were nearly two and a half times more likely to lose interest in sex.[51]

"The impact of relationship duration is something that comes up constantly," says Lori Brotto, a psychologist at the University of British Columbia who works with women diagnosed with what's been called hypoactive sexual-desire disorder—meaning they're just not feeling desire for their partner. "Sometimes I wonder whether it isn't so much about libido as it is about boredom."[52]

That's what a 2014 study led by University of Alaska Southeast associate psychology professor Ali Ziegler, "Does Monogamy Harm Women? Deconstructing Monogamy with a Feminist Lens," found as well. In addition to noting that there's nothing about monogamy that works particularly well for women sexually (although having a partner around to help raise children may be desirable), for many women diagnosed with hypoactive sexual-desire disorder, the loss of interest in sex is often because of mismatched sexual desire between monogamous partners, not a "problem" specific to her.[53]

Despite what many experts say about women being better suited for monogamy than men, research indicates that isn't the case, whether the woman is heterosexual, lesbian, or bisexual.[54]

So, what, if anything, can women do? What Klusmann found

in his surveys is illuminating—women who lived apart from their romantic partner tended to keep their desire longer. Absence not only seems to make the heart grow fonder, it also makes the libido stronger.

But absence also means you don't have any idea what your partner's up to. Some people worry that if you're not living with each other, well, they're likely to act on their desire with someone else. Are LATs more likely to cheat on each other?

Again, we turn to science.

Enjoying greater freedom in a romantic relationship while also expecting monogamy, which many LATs assume, requires a certain amount of trust.[55]

Some recent studies indicate that missing your partner may actually make you feel more connected to each other and even *more* faithful.[56] As sociologist Eva Illouz notes in her 2012 book, *Why Love Hurts*, LAT relationships help us cope with the ontological insecurities that come with romantic relationships. We are basically forced to contend with all our insecurities, and that can lead to greater introspection and self-awareness.[57]

That doesn't mean that couples who don't live together don't cheat on each other. Some do. Of course, infidelity occurs even when couples live together, so it's less about *how* you structure your living arrangement and more about *whom* you structure your living arrangement with.

It's about trust—essential to any relationship—and communication. Living with your partner doesn't guarantee that you'll be excellent communicators, evidenced by the thousands of articles and dozens of books published yearly offering tips for couples on how to communicate better. What recent research indicates is that couples tend to feel more satisfied with their relationship when there was less negative communication than usual, which makes sense (oddly, positive communication didn't do all that much to boost satisfaction).[58]

For LAT couples, communication isn't always face-to-face. It often relies on technology—texts, video calls, etc.—as well as phone calls and sometimes mailed letters and cards when couples aren't together. Not to say there isn't negative communication if you're not living together, but one study of couples in long-distance relationships found that they learned how to communicate better and gained valuable relationship skills, including trust, patience, time management, independence, and intimacy that wasn't just about sex and touch. And they were less likely to take their partner for granted.[59] Those skills can help couples feel more committed to each other, and if you feel committed to each other, you're more motivated to act in ways that your partner experiences as loving.

Another study found that, in addition to higher levels of satisfaction, more love for their partner, more positive reminiscences about their partner, and higher levels of perceived agreement with their partner than couples who lived closer to each other, they also experienced "better communication quality."[60]

Finally, many couples who live together often stay together even if they don't really want to simply because it may be too much for them to deal with.[61] Of course, there also is pressure from others—family, friends, and society—to not only want to *be* in a stable long-term partnership, but also to *maintain* it once they have one, as well as internalized pressure.[62]

As Joel notes, couples who live apart don't have the same constraints that couples who live together have, where breaking up and having to move out might be a hassle emotionally, physically, and financially, so it's easy for them to feel more confident that they are in the relationship for the right reasons, not because they have few options.[49]

THE BAD STUFF

Now, to the negatives. As I mentioned above, there are a few. Again, from the chapter on LATs in *The New I Do*, here are the biggies:[63]

- You may face judgment and misunderstanding from family, friends, and coworkers.
- It may create emotional distress or uncertainty.
- It can be expensive.
- It can be complicated if you're raising your children together.
- It may be lonely at times.
- You may differ on how much time you should spend apart.
- You may differ on how you'll spend time together.
- It may not feel comfortable relying on the phone, video apps, email, or other technology to catch up with each other daily.
- You might feel jealous and/or suspicious.
- You may feel a lack of control.
- You and your partner may not be able to have intercourse when you both want it.
- It may be challenging to make joint decisions from afar.
- If you're living apart because of circumstance and not choice, you may feel frustrated and resentful.
- You may start to grow apart.
- You may feel like your relationship is less "we" and "us" focused.
- If you only have limited time together, you may avoid bringing up certain issues that need to be addressed.

- You may feel anxiety.
- You may feel guilt.
- It may be harder to solve disagreements.

Of course, some if not all of those experiences also occur within live-together relationships. Many cohabiting couples grow apart, thus the rise in "gray divorce" among those age fifty and older, the only ages that are experiencing more divorces; many don't always agree on when to have sex, which is why twenty-six percent of married couples under the age of sixty say they had sex once a month or less in 2021, according to the 2021 General Social Survey[64]; many feel jealous or suspicious, or both; and many are even lonely together. In 2018, the Pew Research Center found that twenty-eight percent of people who are dissatisfied with their family life feel lonely all or most of the time,[65] and the 2021 General Social Survey indicates about fourteen percent of married couples are not very happy.[66]

But let's get to Professor Simon Duncan's findings. Duncan says there's a "darker motivation" by people, especially women, who are choosing to be LATs. "[P]eople can end up living apart because they feel anxious, vulnerable, even fearful about living with a partner," he writes.[67]

Of course, as Ingrid Arnet Connidis, Klas Borell, and Sofie Ghazanfareeon Karlsson note in their 2017 study on ambivalence in older LAT partners, "Seeing such vulnerability or constraint as motivators unique to LAT also ignores the reality that many women (and men) enter marriage for similar reasons."[68]

Using a nationwide British survey supplemented by fifty interviews, twenty-nine of whom were women, Duncan finds that, rather than creating a better type of romantic relationship, many couples—typically older—would prefer to live together but are choosing to live apart because they've been hurt by previous live-together partners, financially as well as emotionally, and some women even experienced abuse. So of course they wouldn't want to replicate that in a new romantic relationship. Maintaining their own spaces is a good way to avoid that.

He also finds that "women, at least in Britain, seldom use LAT to purposefully or reflexively undo gender," as many of the women he interviewed still cook and clean for their male partners.[69]

Other studies, in Sweden and Israel, indicate that LAT couples tend to meet in the woman's home and, yes, the women did the cooking[70] and sometimes even "mothered" their partner's children and extended family.[71] That said, they did it on their own terms, and not every day.

A 2017 study of twenty-two LAT men and women living in the Netherlands also indicated many expressed a fear of commitment and getting hurt.[72] But a lot depended on why the couples were living apart—was it too soon to live together but that was the goal at some point, were they regretfully living apart because of circumstances such as education or work, or were they happily choosing to be LATs? As one might expect, those who happily chose to live separately from their partner didn't think cohabiting would be beneficial to their relationship, and some, especially older people, thought it might even lead to a breakup.

Still, the researchers found that although many said they were deeply emotionally attached to their partner, their "commitment to maintaining their relationship in the future was less strong and clear-cut. . . . The notion of a life-long partnership was generally not valued very highly," especially for those who were older and more experienced in life, love, and the inevitability of breakups.

Those findings seem to corroborate two other studies, a 2017 study of LATs in the United States and a 2014 study comparing French, German, Australian, and Russian LATs.

The US study by sociologist Alisa C. Lewin compared LAT relationships with first marriages, remarriages, and cohabitation among adults aged fifty-seven to eighty-five.[73] She discovered that people in live apart together relationships experienced less support—although they didn't expect they'd have support—and were less happy, but they also had less strain, possibly because providing support and attempting to control things like a partner's health behaviors can burden a relationship.

In the study of four countries, LAT couples without plans to marry or live together within the next three years were the least satisfied of those who were married, cohabiting with plans to marry, cohabiting with no plans to marry, and living apart together with plans to marry or cohabit, in most, but not all, of the countries. The researchers also note that LAT men, compared to LAT women, might be less satisfied in their relationships than married or cohabiting men because they may be missing out on women's unpaid labor and caregiving. Now you can understand why some women prefer LAT![74]

That's what journalist Zosia Bielski discovered.

In her 2019 article in *The Globe and Mail* titled "The new reality of dating over 65: Men want to live together; women don't," Bielski cited the research of sociologists Karen Kobayashi and Laura Funk, who interviewed heterosexual couples aged sixty-five and older living in Canada, where nine percent of the population lives apart from their romantic partner.[75] Their study indicated that men often assumed they'd eventually move in with their female partners, but the women did not, unwilling to give up their freedom and give in to the "structural commitments"—you can read into that what you will—of cohabitating relationships.[76]

The article attracted more than five hundred comments, which garnered a follow-up article, titled "'Don't trade your pension for a prostate.' Readers react to the reality of dating over age sixty-five and women who don't want to live together," which highlighted some of those comments.[77] One woman, in a nod to Duncan's research, wrote, "Living together would be amazing, but I just think it gets harder to find or negotiate harmony and compatibility in a living situation as you age. And when women or men are financially independent (not rich but able to support themselves), living together becomes a choice but not necessary."

Another wrote, "If you're a grouchy old guy who makes little financial contribution, doesn't cook or clean, isn't a ball of fun to be around and looks at women of his own generation as second-best, what are you offering an independent 70-year-old woman who can look after herself? The sexes have become more equal, which means women have more choices. I expect there are also more wealthy and interesting 70-year-old women with 50-year-old boy toys than in the past as well." Which seems to confirm what Bowling Green State University gerontologists Wendy K. Watson and Charlie Stelle found in their 2011 study of why women in their sixties and seventies date. A few things became clear early on—the women wanted companionship but were willing to be lonely before sacrificing their independence.[1]

It could be that a LAT relationship works particularly well for older adults, especially those who are divorced or widowed. According to a 2021 study, eighty-six percent of older people had no expectations to either cohabit or marry and were also less likely to expect marriage than those who lived together. "LAT relationships appear to be long-term partnerships in the United States," the paper concludes.[78]

Because of that, Connidis, Borell, and Karlsson believe future studies of LATs should separate older adults who see the lifestyle as a viable alternative to living with a romantic partner and not as a path to eventual cohabitation. They propose that they be called LLATs, a term for those living apart together in later life.[68]

In her study of twenty fifty-nine- to eighty-nine-year-old LAT men and women, Denise Brothers, director and assistant professor at Madonna University's aging studies program, concludes that LLAT couples were indeed engaging in a new family form, one that allowed them to "redo" gender in a way that they could not achieve in their previous marriages.[79]

As I noted in the introduction, this book is not about presenting LAT relationships as being better than any other kind of romantic relationship, just another option. And as I wrote in the beginning of this chapter, most of us don't turn to studies to determine how to structure our relationships, romantic or not. That said, some people fear being alone, dying alone, and experiencing loneliness, especially as they age.

It isn't all that easy to end a marriage or to even to disentangle a cohabiting relationship, which may up the odds that those couples will stay together even if they're unhappy. It shouldn't work that way for LAT couples, as they don't have the same constraints, observes Chaya Koren of the University of Haifa. Still, Koren writes that numerous studies indicate that older people "may remain in unsatisfactory LAT partnerships because they fear loneliness and perceive being in a relationship as preferable to being alone."[80]

Loneliness and dying alone are beyond the scope of this book. And while it may appear to be more likely that the married and cohabiting couples among us *may* have a loved one nearby at the moment when life changes—whether it's something like a stroke, heart attack, head injury, or death—there's no guarantee that they *will* be there. It's just as likely that a nonromantic partner such as a friend, roommate, coworker, parent, neighbor, or child will be close by at the moment we need them most. Or no one could be there, as is what happened to the late Supreme Court justice Antonin Scalia, who died alone despite having a wife of fifty-six years, nine children, and thirty-six grandchildren.[81] But as singles advocate and author Bella DePaulo writes, do we want to let the final hours of our life dictate how we live our entire life?[82]

That's a question with no right or wrong answer, just one you'll have to answer for yourself.

2 | WHO ARE THESE PEOPLE?

Even if the name Helen Fisher doesn't sound familiar to you, you most likely know of her work, especially if you like reading about the science of love, romance, dating, and attraction. Fisher, a biological anthropologist, best-selling author, and human behavior researcher, is a renowned expert on romantic love and an adviser to the Internet dating site Match.com.

In other words, she knows a lot about love and what it takes to keep it fresh and exciting. So, it's interesting to see what happened when Fisher fell in love, which I detailed in the introduction. She and her new husband, John Tierney, decided to live apart.

"I miss him terribly," she admits, "but it's a great way to have a really long-term romance."[7]

Why? Does the love expert know something the rest of us don't?

For Fisher, what makes her second marriage work after a

short-lived marriage in her twenties and several long relationships is acknowledging and respecting their different interests.

"I like going out with my girlfriends and going to the theater and the opera. I like to go out and I like to walk through the streets of New York. He loves to stay home and read and do his thing," she explains on the podcast *Homegrown Humans*. "What the beauty of that is these days, we can make all different kinds of partnerships."[83]

Journalist and podcaster Diane Rehm also lives apart from her third husband, John Hagedorn—they married in 2017 when she was eighty-one and he was seventy-eight.[84]

"I'm not moving to Florida, and he is not moving to Washington. It will be a modern marriage in the most modern sense of the word," she wrote on her blog.[85]

As she explains on the *Dating While Gray* podcast, he's a retired Lutheran minister who works as a hospital chaplain in West Palm Beach, Florida, and she continues her work in Washington, D.C.[86] "He travels back and forth between West Palm Beach and Washington. He jokes he 'owns' Jet Blue. Our relationship is one of wonderful reunions," she says.[87]

In a September 14, 2022, Facebook post, sixty-eight-year-old author Joyce Maynard—who has had two marriages, one ending in divorce and one ending in death—announced that she does not live with her current partner, Jordan.

"He has a house in Connecticut. I'm in New Hampshire. He plays in a tennis league. I spend long hours at my desk. He likes to watch Yankees games. I don't have a TV. We love each other but we understand—as two people with decades of life experience under our belts—that we have our own separate lives and histories and ways of living."[88]

You may notice that Fisher, Rehm, and Maynard are past midlife and in new relationships after previous marriages that were "traditional," in that they lived with their spouses. Since this chapter is about who is choosing to have a live apart together relationship, let's start there—people in their fifties and older.

As discussed in Chapter 1, the LAT lifestyle is particularly appealing to this demographic, especially if they've been married or in long-term, committed cohabiting relationships before. And, as also previously noted, it is a particularly attractive arrangement for women, who tend to be the ones to insist on it.[89] As Fisher told Tierney when he proposed, "I said, I'll marry you, but I'm not moving in."[83]

While tying the knot mattered to traditional-minded Rehm—Fisher was fine without marrying again, but she knew it mattered to Tierney, and so she agreed[90]—other women at midlife and older have no interest in marrying again, as Cornell Law School professor Cynthia Grant Bowman discovered. In fact, some of the fifty-and-older LAT women she surveyed in the United States and England had rather hostile feelings toward the institution of marriage, and the vast majority either chose to live apart from their romantic partners from the get-go or, after trying it out for a while, decided they preferred it—clearly in conflict with Professor Simon Duncan's findings discussed in Chapter 1.[91]

QUEER BEGINNING

That said, Third Agers—people who are past the age of retirement but haven't yet entered "old age"—and, in particular, middle-aged and older women, aren't the only ones who enjoy the commitment and freedom the LAT lifestyle offers. David Eichert, a PhD candidate in international relations at the London School of Economics and Political Science, also found that it's attractive to some same-sex couples, especially gay men.[92]

As you can imagine, with limited studies on LAT relationships in general, there's even less known about same-sex couples who are choosing to be LATs. Eichert's research indicates that a number of gay men choose to be in LAT relationships for many of the same reasons hetero people say they prefer to live apart—different sleep schedules and levels of cleanliness, a desire for solitude, autonomy, etc.—with one big exception. Many of the gay men he interviewed (a small survey of just fourteen members of ten gay male couples who all lived in New York City, so perhaps not fully representative of gay male LATs) were in an open relationship of some sort,[93] and having separate living spaces helped them practically, because the other partner didn't have to leave during a sexual encounter, as well as emotionally, because it defused the potential for jealousy and wasn't so in-your-face.[94] Obviously, not all gay men are in open relationships. That said, LAT relationships are somewhat more common among gay men than among heterosexual men (perhaps because, as discussed in Chapter 1, hetero men may not want to miss out on their female romantic partner's unpaid labor and caregiving). A LAT lifestyle is also attractive to gay men and lesbian women for reasons that heterosexuals may not experience, studies have found, such as maintaining privacy about their sexual relationships, especially to unaccepting family or in parts of the country where same-sex stigma is still strong (or parts of the world where it's illegal), and because they may not be raising children with a romantic partner and thus need a hands-on coparent.

Same-sex partners also are more likely to seek and achieve more equality in their intimate relationships than heterosexual couples.[95]

This is also what makes LAT relationships attractive for people who identify as solo polyamorists. That's a term that first gained popularity in 2012 through the blog Solopoly.net to describe people who practice ethical nonmonogamy and have multiple meaningful relationships without having a committed primary partner or partners. It's also seen as a rejection of heteronormative relationship standards.[96]

That live apart together arrangements are attractive to people who live outside the heteronormative norms actually has a history—a queer history. While many like to point to famous different-sex LAT couples such as artists Frida Kahlo and her husband, Diego Rivera, who lived in two houses in Mexico City next to each other and connected by a bridge,[97] it was gay men who first embraced the lifestyle.

In his exploration of marriage-like relationships between gay men, sociologist Joseph Harry distributed questionnaires to 241 gay men in the Detroit area in 1975. In his study, "The 'Marital' Liaisons of Gay Men," published in 1979, he noted that many of the men didn't live with their romantic partner. There was an important reason—it was a way to build a committed relationship at a time when same-sex relationships were not universally accepted.[98]

"Maintaining a separate household from one's lover may be a device through which the gay man can avoid awkward situations with and questions from heterosexual friends or relatives. When heterosexuals to whom a gay couple have not 'come out' visit the gay couple's shared residence, awkward questions may arise out of the visible sleeping arrangements," Harry writes.

All these decades later, keeping their private life private still seems to be desirable for many gay men.

As noted in Chapter 1, the Victorians encouraged the idea of spouses sleeping apart in the 1800s. Perhaps they were inspired by the Palace of Versailles, which was transformed by Louis XIV from Louis XIII's glorified hunting lodge in the 1600s to the opulent palace we know today, with separate but identical apartments for the king and queen. Until Louis XIV decided to co-opt some of the queen's space, that is, limiting her to just her State Apartments.[99]

But Louis XIV also had a more modest estate built about a mile from the palace, Grand Trianon, as a private retreat. It was there that Marie Antoinette created a "room" of her own after she was gifted what was known as the Petit Trianon by her husband, Louis XVI, in a nod to her struggles with adapting to court life. Along with gardens, a working farm known as the hamlet, and a "Temple of Love," the Petit Trianon was the place she could escape to for some much-needed me time. She also built a grotto—basically a cave—that had a moss bed and two entrances, "prompting much speculation as to what went on in it," writes journalist Owen Jarus.[100]

Indeed!

Let's face it: not everyone is cut out to live with other people. It doesn't mean they don't want commitment or a caring, loving, romantic, and perhaps sexual relationship.

Sometimes it's due to a matter of personality; some people have higher agentic needs as well as individualistic interests and goals. Sometimes it's due to different cleanliness or neatness levels—my paper piles drove my former husband crazy—or design aesthetics. Sometimes it's due to practicalities—one of you is a night owl, the other an up-and-at-'em early riser. Sometimes, it's due to something you may not have control over—one or the other of you is neurodivergent, or perhaps you or your partner are raising a child or children who are.

In a Reddit community for neurodivergent people, one poster noted that living separately from her partner gave each of them "more space to recharge and having [sic] things the way we both like it. It's a lot of constant compromise when we have different environmental stimulation tolerances. I need calm and [quiet] and he needs loud and busy. We make it work, but I prefer the modern 'living separately together' mentality."[101]

NOT WANTED BUT NECESSARY

There are other practical reasons that prompt couples to live apart, perhaps not always by choice, such as people with disabilities. There are more than eight million people in the United States who receive disability benefits, either through Supplemental Security Income or Disabled Adult Child or both, and who would lose benefits or have them severely reduced if they married, according to the Disability Rights Education & Defense Fund. This, of course, could prevent couples who might prefer a more traditional arrangement from putting a ring on it and living together.[102] But as we'll see in Chapter 7, couples with disabilities in the United States don't need to marry or live together to potentially lose their benefits or have them severely reduced.

In Sweden, where more than five percent of couples are LATs, living with a romantic partner could reduce access to public social services, penalizing older people who would like to marry or at least live together.[103]

In South Korea, more couples are becoming what's called "weekend couples"—another name for commuter couples—living apart from their spouses and children because of their careers during the week and coming together on weekends, although the decision isn't always a happy one.[104]

Living apart from one's romantic partner also seems to be attractive to people who have children from previous relationships. Many people are exhausted just by thinking about melding families and trying to re-create something akin to the popular 1970s TV show *The Brady Bunch*, in which widower Mike Brady, played by Robert Reed, and a woman, Carol Martin, played by Florence Henderson—the show never explained if Carol was divorced, widowed, a single mother by choice, or some sort of baby mama, although that's highly unlikely given the era—marry and move in together with his three sons and her three daughters.

It's one thing if it's a TV sitcom and any sibling kerfuffles are resolved by the end of the episode; it's quite another thing to make it work in real life.

"Trying to fully blend families can be hard," Mandi Kreitel shared with *The Wall Street Journal.* She and her husband have children from previous marriages and live 360 miles apart in Alaska. In addition to having different parenting styles—"I'm definitely a disciplinarian. He's definitely more fun"—they each share custody with their former spouses, making moving in together or even closer to each other a real challenge.[105]

Even if custody isn't shared with a former spouse for whatever reason, or there isn't a former spouse or coparent, many parents don't want to move their children away from their schools, neighborhoods, friends, and perhaps extended family. And in the United States, the red state–blue state divide may prevent some people from moving to the state where their partner lives.

Other people can't or don't want to live with a new partner because of their strong feelings of responsibility toward their elderly parents, whether they live with them or not. If they moved away from them and couldn't visit or care for them as often and easily, it could mean that at some point their parents might have to move into an assisted living facility.[27]

All these are important reasons some people choose to not live together. And then there's one that impacts many more people.

SOME ZZZS, PLEASE

Finally, let's talk about sleep. As in, many of us don't get enough of it.

In 2016, *Huffington Post* (now *HuffPost*) founder Arianna Huffington started calling herself a "sleep evangelist."[106] It wasn't something she had imagined for herself, but when she fainted, exhausted from eighteen-hour days spent building the news website, and woke up bloody with a broken cheekbone and a cut over her eye that required reconstructive surgery and months of recovery, she took it as a wake-up call.[107]

Huffington wrote *The Sleep Revolution: Transforming Your Life, One Night at a Time* and launched the website Thrive Global, with a focus on sleep and wellness, to alert people to the dangers of being sleep-deprived. Although she acknowledges in her book that it's time to get rid of the stigma against couples sleeping in separate rooms as if it's some sign that they are in marital trouble,[108] she doesn't mention it as an option in her twelve tips for better sleep.[109]

Thankfully, someone wrote a whole book about that.

In *Sleeping Apart Not Falling Apart*, Jennifer Adams offers the history and science of sleep as well as practical advice for people who find that sleeping in the same bed as their romantic partner— no matter how much they expected and wanted to—is keeping them from getting their much-needed rest. So, it's no surprise that living apart together would be an attractive alternative, whether in separate rooms in one space or separate spaces.

"Considering all the emotional and physical benefits of sleep, the sum of two healthy/rested individuals who make up a loving couple are greater than their individual parts," Eric Marlowe Garrison, a certified sex counselor and chair of the American Association of Sex Educators, Counselors and Therapists, tells *The Washington Post*.[110]

It's particularly important to women, new research finds. Women are more likely to experience insomnia and restless leg syndrome, and, as they age, obstructive sleep apnea, all of which can impact their mental health.[111]

Having two primary bedroom suites was named the "hottest new amenity in luxury homes" in 2017 by *Architectural Digest*.[112] Clients were either transforming spaces in an existing unit into a second suite or adding it to the designs of a new unit. "Just as technology evolves, so do people," says Ralph Choeff, of the Miami-based architecture and design firm Choeff Levy Fischman. "I would say it's an evolution of not only sleeping habits but bathroom habits, work schedules, and simply personal space that most of our clients frankly can afford."

Still, the stigma about sleeping apart from your sweetie is strong, a topic we'll dive into in a future chapter.

One thing is clear—people who are choosing to be LATs have to be more intentional and creative in their relationship. There's no downside to that in my mind.

In their 2001 paper "Dual Dwelling Duos: An Alternative for Long-term Relationships," therapists Judye Hess and Padma Catell acknowledge that society's expectations about what relationships look like don't work for everyone. And that has real-life ramifications.

"As therapists we are confronted every day with people who are dealing with relationship problems. It seems that many people are trying to fit themselves into a very narrow model for long-term relationship [sic] that does not work well for their personalities," they write. "Believing that there is only one healthy way to have long-term relationships, and repeatedly failing at it, leads to a lot of pain and to repeated feelings of failure for one or both of the partners."[113]

Many people feel like failures when they can't make a "traditional" relationship model work. Worse, they often think there's something wrong with them and rarely consider that it could be the actual model that's wrong—for them.

On a 2022 episode of the *Dating While Gray* podcast, the twice-divorced Gia admits that the longer she's remained single, the less she's interested in sharing a home with someone without boundaries, envisioning what her daughter Lauryn calls a "butterfly house," "where everybody has their own everything on this side, and their own everything on this side, and they, like, have dates in the middle."[114]

If any of this resonates with you, perhaps you, too, will be one of "these people."

3 | IT'S NOT JUST FOR THE RICH AND OTHER MYTHS

Telling friends and family that you've met someone wonderful and you have no intention of living with them is likely to get one response: "What is wrong with you?" After all, when you are in love with someone, you live together, right?

Not always, as we've already explored.

It's not all that uncommon for couples to spend huge swaths of time apart because of their careers, whether they are in the military or work as firefighters, pilots and flight attendants, long-haul truck drivers, and CEOs, among others. In other words, we don't have a problem when people live apart from their romantic partner because they made a decision to have a career that *requires* them to be away, perhaps because we understand that, at some point, they'll return home. But to *choose* to be away from a loved one for any other reason? It's harder to wrap our heads around it.

And to live apart after you've already lived together? Something must be wrong—you're obviously on the way to a breakup, less committed, not really in love, are selfish and self-absorbed, avoidant, and most likely fooling around on the side or hoping to.

We've already seen how those narratives aren't true, but it is one of the big myths about couples who choose to live apart.

Not everyone who is a LAT is married, but we can glean a lot from what people say about LAT marriages. I can't tell you how many times I've heard people ask, "Why even get married if you're going to live apart?"

Except people get married for lots of reasons besides love, the top reason heterosexual couples cite for tying the knot, according to the Pew Research Center. They also mention lifelong commitment, companionship, children, having the relationship be recognized by a religious ceremony, financial stability, and, finally, legal rights and benefits[115] (same-sex couples overwhelmingly say the legal rights and protections are the main reason they want to wed).[116]

No one mentions living together as a reason to wed, although it's probably just assumed. Interestingly, all the stated reasons for marrying can also be achieved while living apart from your romantic partner, including companionship. Remember what psychology professor and author Eli J. Finkel says about having "other significant others" (OSO)—family, neighbors, coworkers, and friends who can be great companions. You don't have to be around one person 24-7 to have companionship.

All that matters is finding a happy, healthy balance of couple time, OSO time, and alone time that works for you as a couple.

Now, about those other myths.

IT'S ONLY FOR THE WEALTHY

One of the biggest myths about LAT relationships is that they are only for those of financial means. As we saw in Chapter 1, all romantic couples start off living in separate households, whether solo or with parents, friends, roommates, or some other configuration. Nothing about their living situation has to change just because they found someone they want to be romantic and potentially sexual with. They can just stay put.

True, it is indeed cheaper to live together under one roof. Pooling resources usually boosts the economic situation of each person. If there's only one mortgage or rental payment, one utility bill, one set of kitchenware, and one household full of furnishings, all that extra money can go toward savings, investments, vacations, or other necessities or indulgences. However, there are other costs involved besides just financial costs, such as potentially having to live farther away from your own social network of family and friends.

The bigger problem with couples who move in together to pool resources, as mentioned earlier, is that they're turning a romantic decision into a financial decision.

And let's not forget that unmarried couples who live together tend to break up more frequently than married couples, especially younger couples.[117] Whether you're married or not, a breakup generally means one or both will have to move out of the shared housing and find a new place to live anyway. A breakup can negatively impact your housing situation in ways that may last for years, especially for women, who tend to make less money than men. Not to say that we should enter a romantic relationship expecting that it will end in a breakup—many do not. Still, it's a possibility that should be acknowledged.

In their study of LATs in France and Italy, demographers Arnaud Régnier-Loilier and Daniele Vignoli suggest that "there is a higher likelihood of being in a LAT relationship when individuals experience economic difficulties," such as those who are contract workers or unemployed, especially among young LATs.[118]

Perhaps the bigger issue is people need to be able to support themselves as is.

"You have to take care of yourself. You have to be able to afford your own lifestyle," psychologist Sherrie Sims Allen, who lived on opposite coasts from her partner and then husband, Melvin, for five years before they moved in together, tells me.[119]

If you're worried about affording a place of your own, there are, of course, things that can be done to help relieve the financial burden, such as moving in with others or renting out a spare room (if you have one) on a temporary basis, such as through services such as Airbnb or VRBO, or on a more permanent basis, such as getting a roommate. There are many home-sharing services that will match you with potential roommates, including *Golden Girls*–like arrangements, shared housing for single moms, and cross-generational roommates.

Living with a roommate isn't the same as living with a romantic partner—you're not sharing the same bed and you don't have the same expectations from them, and it's often the heightened expectations from romantic partners that cause a lot of resentments, frustrations, and anger.

THEY'RE MORE LIKELY TO CHEAT

It's true—sometimes people who live apart from each other cheat on their partner. But so do people who live together. It's hard to know how many people fool around on their romantic partners—rates of infidelity are self-reported, and not everyone admits to being a cheater—but since many more couples live together than live apart, it's obvious that living together doesn't prevent anyone from having an affair.

Still, it could be that living apart makes cheating easier. After all, there is a lot more time spent alone, often in separate places, and it would be much easier to hide any extradyadic shenanigans. Plus, while people might love the freedom of having their own space, they may also feel lonely from time to time, and lonely people may find themselves in a situation they didn't expect.

One of the many things live apart together relationships can do is help people cope with the uncertainties that come with romantic relationships. If you're not around your partner all the time, you may not know their friends and coworkers all that well, if at all. You may not know how they're spending their time, where, and with whom.

That doesn't automatically mean your partner is going to be unfaithful. In fact, one study indicates that missing your romantic partner can actually make you feel *more* faithful.[120]

Clearly, being in a LAT relationship forces you to face your insecurities and your level of trust.[121] For some people, that can lead to greater introspection and self-awareness; for others, it may cause anxiety.

While those choosing a LAT relationship may not end up having an affair any more or less than those who live together, they may think about it more. And that may prompt them to have more conversations about monogamy and infidelity, which can't hurt and actually might help.

"Our society is obsessed with cheating and infidelity, I believe in large part because people don't actually take the time to discuss what their boundaries are—when you decide to be exclusive, when you go to a next level, whatever it is. You have to sit down and decide, how do we want to feel, and how do we want to be when the other is not around, what is allowed and what isn't. If you don't talk about it, then it's easier to get thrown off by a boundary violation," says therapist Heather "Lulu" Mazzei, who practices solo polyamory and is a LAT.[122]

"It's your responsibility to help your partner feel secure in the relationship. If your partner's not feeling secure, you have to ask yourself, 'What am I doing or not doing that's causing them to feel this way?'" she says. "I keep coming back to this: communication takes work, relationships take work, no matter what kind of relationship. You have to ask yourself, 'What kind of work do I want to put in?'"

That's the discussion Elaine Romero, a therapist who cohosts the *Love Is in the Air* podcast with her husband, Abe, had. Each of them dealt with betrayals in their previous marriages, and since she lives in California and he lives in Texas, they worked hard to build trust in the seven years they've been a couple, five as husband and wife.

"A huge part of it would have to be a lot of dialogue in the beginning, to say, 'Here are my needs and thoughts on that. Are you willing to sign up for this?' You can have that initial dialogue, but then things come up as you go, 'What's making me feel safe and what's not making me feel safe?'" she says.

"It's not so much I'm scared of him cheating on me, because if he cheats on me, I know what the plan is." (She'd end the relationship ASAP.)

"What's more of what I need from him is to help me feel safe along the way. I'm in a relationship where if I get scared, there's space and room for me to tell him I'm scared, and . . . there's space and room for us to have a dialogue about how to make it more comfortable for me, how to make it more comfortable for him," she says. "The decisions we make aren't Elaine's rules for Abe or Abe's rules for Elaine; we make mutual decisions, a plan, our plan together . . . what we both feel comfortable with."[123]

Ultimately, it comes down to this: Are you with someone you trust, and is that person worthy of your trust? And are you someone your partner can trust? If you can't trust your partner and they can't trust you, whatever living arrangement you have isn't going to change the situation. It isn't *how* you live—together or apart—it's *whom* you are with.

IT'S SELFISH

"Just when you think America's 'all about me' culture has peaked—one finds out there is so much more room for more 'me,'" conservative journalist Betsy Hart began her 2006 column on live apart together relationships, titled, "'Living apart together' relationship ultimately selfish."[124]

"[O]ne of the beautiful things about marriage is precisely that it calls us—or should call us—to a sense of 'other,' of connecting to and living for something bigger and more important than just ourselves, of learning to sacrifice and give and share and live and receive in a way that makes us human," she writes. "[C]an these willful, permanently separate, overtly minimalist relationships be true relationships? Answer: No."

Actually, the answer is yes, therapists Judye Hess and Padma Catell would say. They acknowledge that many therapists consider LATs—what they call dual-dwelling duos—as "a condition to be cured, rather than a legitimate life style [*sic*] option." But, as they point out, there's no reason to believe that living together as a family "reflects a more advanced developmental stage."[113]

Calling LATs selfish is an offshoot of the narrative that singles in general are somehow selfish, something social scientist Bella DePaulo, PhD, has been pushing back on since before her book *Singled Out: How Singles Are Stereotyped, Stigmatized, and Ignored, and Still Live Happily Ever After* was published in 2004.

Relying on numerous studies, DePaulo has found that singles not only aren't selfish—they're actually *more* generous with their time, money, and caregiving than married people are.[125]

Similarly, LATs "make room in their hearts and their lives for friends. They are especially likely to have one, or even more than one, friend they can confide in. They are more likely than the people in any of the other groups to have gotten help from a friend when they needed it (though the rates were high for the others as well). They don't regard their friends dismissively, as just people to have fun with. They don't seem to worry that their own friendships—or their own careers, for that matter—will threaten their romantic relationships," she writes.[126]

Still, anytime someone prioritizes their independence—which is one reason some people are drawn to living apart together—it can cause others to feel resentful of them. Why do they need all that freedom? What are they actually doing with all that freedom? This seems to be particularly bothersome if those seeking independence are women, especially if they're using their free time for leisure instead of how society prefers women to act—in the service of others.[127]

That expectation may cause some women to alter what they want to do in their free time to accommodate what their romantic partner wants, meaning that "their leisure activities are less in line with their own preferences and thus less enjoyable."[128]

As we've already seen, many midlife and older women who embrace living apart together are not interested in having less-enjoyable free time (and many still prioritize spending their free time with their adult children and grandchildren over their LAT partner). That's hardly being selfish.

Yet that's how women in LAT relationships often see themselves, even describing their way of living as "self-centered," whereas the men in LAT relationships did not. Tellingly, the women were not interested in changing a thing, as many believe that they had to put the needs of others first in previous relationships and they were done with that.[129]

"Sure, some will say by insisting on places of their own, they are behaving selfishly. But what if instead, by tending to their own places and their own spaces, they are nurturing their souls? And what if that attentiveness to their own needs is an expansive act rather than an isolating one?" asks DePaulo. "What if that very self-care is what makes it possible for them to care deeply about partners and about other people, too, and maybe even save their marriages along the way?"[130]

YOU'RE JUST DATING

Look in the comment section of almost any article on live apart together relationships and you'll see a common opinion: "you're just dating," or some variation on the theme.

Montreal filmmaker Sharon Hyman, who has been mentioned previously, has lived apart from her romantic partner for more than two decades. She runs a Facebook page for LATs and is making a documentary film on the lifestyle, which she cleverly calls "apartners," and she has heard it all. "You're just friends with benefits" is a typical judgment.

Her response: "It's been more than 23 years. Those are some benefits! I don't know too many casual daters who are the executors of each other's estates and have each other's powers of attorney," she writes in a first-person essay in *Time* magazine.[131]

It is true—some LAT couples consider themselves to be "just dating" and not an established couple, but there are many LAT couples who are what Professor Simon Duncan and Miranda Phillips call "partner LATs."[132] And many partner LAT couples like Hyman are deeply enmeshed in each other's lives. Not all LATs may make their partner the executor of their estate or have each other's powers of attorney, especially if they have children from previous relationships. But that begs the question—what actions are needed to be considered a "real" couple to others? Is it truly based on sharing a living space 24–7? Or is it the commitment and loving behavior the people in the relationship express? And, who gets to decide what a real couple looks like?

Many people have questioned the marriages of couples who live together but have huge age differences, such as the thirty-nine-year difference between actor Dennis Quaid and Laura Savoie, who married in 2020 when he was sixty-six and she was twenty-seven. If couples can follow all the rules that make others feel comfortable—marry and live together—but an age difference still causes that relationship to be questioned, what's the problem? Living together? The age difference? Both?

YOU CAN'T RAISE KIDS TOGETHER

My children were nine and twelve years old when their father and I divorced. We had a fifty-fifty hands-on coparenting agreement—a week with their dad and a week with me. I'll admit, my boys would have preferred to continue living in one house with their parents and not have to travel back and forth—a few blocks from each other, but still. But they had two parents who loved them, and who would gather together for birthdays, holidays, their sports events, graduations, and other celebrations, as well as having comfy rooms in each house. This, of course, was not unique just to my family; there are thousands of divorced parents who offer similar loving arrangements.

It's perhaps unusual to think of a divorced family as being a model for coparenting when the parents don't live together but are very much a couple, and yet in many ways it is.

If they're doing it right, parents will sit down with their children and explain in age-appropriate language what's happening, what it will look like, and what to expect, and they will consider their children's opinions and desires in shaping the new arrangement.

There are many children being raised with one parent at home and one who commutes for work and only comes back to the family home for short visits, or who is deployed overseas, or is incarcerated, or any configuration that keeps them apart for lengths of time.

Then there are people like CNN political commentator Van Jones, who had a daughter with his longtime friend—not his romantic partner—in February 2022 and who plans to raise her "as coparenting partners."[133] They do not live together.

According to a 2018 post by the nonpartisan, research-based center Zero to Three, "Kids don't grow up in perfect worlds, nor do they need to. What children do need are parents who, whether living together or not, demonstrate respect for each other, communicate calmly and without anger, and who make their child's needs the central focus of their decision-making."[134]

And that can happen in any kind of living arrangement, as we'll see in Chapter 8, which goes with much more depth into the hows of raising a child or children together while living apart.

IT'S WASTEFUL

Among the many concerns people have about the rise in solo living is how harmful it is to the environment compared with multiple people living in one household. LATs aren't solo, per se, as they have a romantic partner and thus are couples (except for people who consider themselves polyamorists or solo polyamorists), but a similar complaint can be made against LATs unless they live with others, such as a family member or roommates.

And there's research that would appear to confirm that harm.[135]

It's true that many housing units, whether a 250-square-foot studio or a 2,500-square-foot single-family house, have their own appliances—stoves, fridges, possibly dishwashers, washers, and dryers—and heating and cooling systems. All that has impacts on the environment.

More important, however, is how the people in those units

actually live, and the studies "proving" solo living is wasteful typically don't take that into account. If you're a family of two, three, or four in one household, yes, you are sharing resources and, yes, that can be better for the environment. But if that family often flies for work or vacations, drives gas-guzzling luxury cars or SUVs, eats out often at high-end restaurants (which is incredibly wasteful),[136] dines on beef a few times a week (cows contribute hugely to greenhouse gases), and has remodeled their perfectly fine kitchen or bathroom, or maybe both, to keep up with new decor trends, their carbon footprint will likely be much higher than that of a solo dweller who lives minimally; who walks, bikes, uses mass transit, or has an electric vehicle; shops at consignment and resale stores; and is vegetarian or vegan.

Plus, some LATs who live close enough to each other often share things that aren't needed on a daily basis, such as tools, lawn mowers, garden implements, vacuum cleaners, and other such household essentials.

Lifestyle matters.

There's just one study that explores the environmental impacts of eco-conscious singles' lifestyles compared with those of conventional singles. Although it was a small study, the findings indicate that the purposeful attempts by eco-minded singles to reduce their impact on the environment are quite significant, leading the researcher to state, "Conclusively, singlehood and solo living cannot be automatically considered as environmentally unfriendly."[137]

If you aren't living as green a lifestyle as you can as a LAT, it's not a bad idea to consider ways to be more eco-minded. If you already are, however, feel free to carry on living apart with a clear conscience.

4 | "HONEY, WE NEED TO TALK."

I was already out of my family home and living on my own when my parents decided to live apart. Actually, I don't think was a mutual decision; I'm pretty sure it was my mother's idea, given what she told me decades later when I asked her how she ended up buying a condo in Miami and living in it on her own with my dad remaining in our modest house in Queens, New York—"I'd had enough."

I also don't know what was said, when it was said, and how it was said. I wish I had thought to ask her, because many years later, living apart from a romantic partner was something I embraced—at first reluctantly—after my second divorce.

Now when I meet someone of potential romantic interest, I make it very clear from the beginning that I don't want to marry again, and I don't want to live with anyone, either, at least for now (never say never, as they say). If they balk at either, I know we're not a good fit, and it's better to know that sooner than later.

But bringing up the idea of being a committed romantic couple and living separately isn't always an easy conversation, especially if your romantic partner talks about living together one day, or expects to live together at some point, or is pressuring you to live together, or if you've already been living together and now want to shake things up. Especially if you think this may be a deal-breaker for them and you don't want to lose them. Especially if, unlike me, you're not one hundred percent sure it's what you should be doing, or, even if you are, you fear the judgment of others.

So, how do you go about it?

"I think the most important word that comes to mind is *gently*," says Heather "Lulu" Mazzei, a therapist based in Los Angeles who practices solo polyamory and is a LAT.[122]

"No matter where you are in your relationship, you have to remember that if you are deciding to be in any kind of coupleship, you are in the care of your partner," she says. "If you're already living together, even more care is required in this conversation, because it's going to throw a wrench in there."

For journalist Diane Rehm, whom we met in Chapter 2, there really wasn't much of a discussion at all when she decided to marry again and she and her new husband had their own homes in different states, she tells me in an email. "We each like our own homes. I don't like Florida. He does like Washington. There was never a long discussion, it was just assumed we would keep our own domiciles."[138]

There wasn't much of a discussion for Jacky Vallée and her LAT partner of some fifteen years, either. "When we started dating, she was in a domestic relationship with someone else (we are polyamorous) and when that relationship ended, we already knew that we were not domestically compatible. So, there was no big decision to make," Vallée writes in an email. "It was more of a decision by omission, so to speak. There was no overt decision not to live together. Neither one of us brought up the possibility." [139]

Part of that was driven by the fact that Vallée had a child at home and her partner isn't interested in having or raising children; they have different ideas on money, cleaning, messes, and other things involved in running a household—and, just as important, her partner had never lived by herself before, and Vallée acknowledges it was important for her to have her own space.

Over the years they have had many opportunities to agree that the "decision by omission" was the right way to go. "Whenever the topic would come up, it was more like, 'Wow, it's a good thing we don't live together.' If we lived together, she would be constantly disappointed by my relative lack of engagement, and I would be constantly annoyed by the persistent expectation to engage."

Still, assuming you and your new romantic partner aren't going to live together is not the best idea. Nor is allowing a decision to be made by omission and not bringing up your expectations, both as an individual and as a couple. And it's important to keep having those conversations throughout the relationship.

"For any type of relationship, communication is key," Mazzei says. "Communication, whether you're in a LAT relationship or not, is not something you ever get to stop working on."

IS IT A *REAL* RELATIONSHIP?

When he was interviewed by *The New York Times* in 2013, art director Rolf Sjogren admitted having complicated feelings about living apart from Robert Fontanelli, whom he'd been in a relationship with for about six years. Each had their own affordable units in not-so-affordable Manhattan, and they were hesitant to give them up.[140]

Still, there was some ambivalence. "Sometimes I wonder, what's wrong with me that I don't live with my partner," Sjogren lamented. He also was exhausted by having to go back and forth between apartments. However, if living apart maintains their relationship, he doesn't see a compelling reason to change anything. "People say it's not real if you don't live together, but I can't imagine it being any realer than this."

Sjogren isn't the only one who has felt the sting of judgment from others for not having a "real" relationship. Couples who don't have what we consider the obvious markers of coupledom—sharing a last name, having children together, or living together, whether married or not—may invite questions.

The question I got when I was with my former partner of nearly eight years—the first serious relationship I had after my second divorce—was "Are you ever going to get married or live together or something like that?"

I didn't have the language to explain what and why we were doing what we were doing at the time, but now, after two decades of living quite happily by myself, it's easier for me to say that I don't want to live with a romantic partner. At least not yet.

That, of course, makes me suspect—what's wrong with me for not wanting to cohabit?

And that's how it's been with those who study LATs, parsing out who has a real relationship—defined as one that's "committed" and "mature"—note the authors of a 2014 paper, "Living Apart Relationships in Contemporary Europe: Accounts of Togetherness and Apartness." But the paper's lead author, Mariya Stoilova, of the London School of Economics and Political Science, wanted to be more inclusive of the many ways people create their intimate relationships. She prefers to call them living apart relationships (LARs). The term *living apart together* puts too much emphasis on "the 'togetherness' of the relationship."[141]

This is important for people whose romantic relationships don't fall into the norm—those who identify as solo poly, for instance, or who don't necessarily prioritize their romantic relationship over their platonic ones.

Stoilova acknowledges that even those who consciously chose to live apart and were quite satisfied with that decision still "had to undergo a long process of adjustment to what they regarded as a 'legitimate' form of intimacy." That caused one middle-aged woman quoted in their paper to question why she and her partner weren't like other couples. Not living together seemed to indicate more of a "failed relationship" than one that actually gave her and her partner exactly what they wanted.

San Francisco Bay Area clinical psychologist Judye Hess, who has lived apart from her partner for more than twenty-four years, acknowledges that couples who choose that lifestyle often receive "less recognition from society for the value or seriousness of their relationship."[142]

They're also seen as being commitmentphobic and less relationship-oriented, Hess complains—a narrow and punitive view of what human relationships can and should be.

"[S]ociety plays an extraordinarily powerful role and therefore, how a third person views us is extremely important," a fiftysomething man in a LAT relationship told sociologists Bernadette Bawin-Legros and Anne Gauthier. "[B]eing a couple is also being recognized as a couple by others. It's automatic for married people. They might not even think of themselves as a couple and still be considered a couple by society . . . [T]he fact that we live separately denies society of one of its most powerful signs, which is the identification of the common domicile. This means that the free couple, living in separate quarters, seeks nonetheless signs of recognition."[143]

So, it's no surprise that, without the support of others, some people might feel ambivalent about the arrangement.

That said, many people often feel ambivalent about a lot of lifestyle choices that do get societal support, from becoming a parent to getting married. According to a 2005 working paper on the meaning of marriage to young adults in the US, many indicated that they felt ambivalent about tying the knot, in part because there are now numerous alternatives to it, an awareness that many marriages end in divorce, and that the bar of what makes a "successful marriage" seems to be raised all the time.[144]

Ambivalence isn't all that bad. In fact, implicit ambivalence—having both strong positive and negative feelings toward your spouse—can actually motivate you to work toward solving whatever conflicts you're having and improve your relationship.[145]

There's ambivalence among those who live together, too, who, although increasingly common among couples, doesn't get the same societal support as those who tie the knot. As historian Elizabeth Pleck writes in her 2012 book *Not Just Roommates: Cohabitation After the Sexual Revolution*, cohabitation was long considered a "poor people's marriage,"[146] and even today, "cohabiters form a second tier of citizens"[147] under federal law. In some states, landlords can refuse to rent to an unmarried couple and cohabitors lose out on all the rights and privileges that go to married couples, such as the right to be covered by a spouse's health insurance and get their Social Security benefits after their death. Plus, couples in heterosexual relationships sometimes have different expectations of living together. Women often tend to see cohabitation as leading to marriage; men, however, don't always see it that way.[148]

In other words, no matter if you're living together but aren't married, or married and living together, or married and living apart, or not married and living apart, ambivalence is baked into romantic relationships. So, ambivalence alone is not a reason to worry about having a LAT relationship.

THE RIGHT WORDS, THE RIGHT TIME

When Lise Stoessel realized her marriage just wasn't working for her, even after years of couples' and individual counseling, she told her husband that she wanted to try living apart as a way to salvage their partnership (a topic that we'll explore in more depth in Chapter 11)—something she'd given a lot of thought to. First up, how to say it.

"I had to get to a place within myself where I wasn't feeling angry, I wasn't feeling bitter, I wasn't feeling fed up or vindictive. I was really feeling like this is going to be a good thing for the two of us; it's going to be a good thing for our family," she tells me.[149] "I was able to bring it up with a positive, and warm, and loving tone, which I think makes all the difference, and very sincere."

She also timed it carefully. She waited until after Father's Day so the family could celebrate together, and, because she's a teacher, after the school year ended for her kids as well as herself.

And as she writes in her 2011 book *Living Happily Ever After—Separately*, she wanted to approach him when she was feeling calm and kind. "I didn't rehearse my lines; I didn't even know exactly what I would say. I just trusted that having worked this for as long as I had, the right words would come out."[150]

She talked about how she was experiencing their married life—she was struggling—and she acknowledged that he also deserved a home life that was without "constant friction, bickering, and resentment."

What Stoessel did was approach the topic with deep compassion and clarity—something Anna Sale, host of the *Death, Sex & Money* podcast, advocates for in her book, *Let's Talk About Hard Things*.

"Hard conversations happen inside relationships, and relationships require their own kind of tending. I believe in kindness and striving for compassion, not spouting off regardless of the pain words can cause," she writes.[151]

When you know you're about to present something that may be tough to talk about—like suggesting to a loved one that you don't want to live together or live together anymore—first do the hard work of understanding *why* you want this arrangement. If you've been living together, ask yourself what's working and what's not, and find the language to express that. Expect that it will be a hard conversation to have, but also expect that it will have a positive outcome (otherwise it most likely won't).[152]

Then comes finding the right time to talk about it. When you're ready, ask your partner to select a good time for them to have an important conversation. When you mutually agree on timing, be clear about what you're struggling with and ask your partner for their experience of your live-in relationship. Sale suggests simple, clear phrases, something like, "What I want has changed."

Then listen—perhaps the hardest part. Listen curiously and empathically.

"You can set yourself up for a more productive, less volatile exchange by being clear about what you are trying to accomplish. This is both the most obvious advice in the world and completely impossible to consistently follow," Sale observes.[153]

When the words finally came out of Stoessel's mouth, that her husband deserved to live in a space that gave him what he needed as much as what she needed, and that she wanted to try living apart, a fundamental shift happened. "For the first time in months, we were able to sit down and have a calm, reasonable talk," she says.[154] He even went to open houses with her to help her find a safe, comfortable place to call her own.

"If you know your partner well enough and you know they'll be upset, you need to prepare for this, but you also need to allow your partner to have their own feelings," says Mazzei.

If you're in the early days of a relationship, your conversation will no doubt be different. Still, Mazzei says, you need to approach it with intention and hold space for whatever your partner feels about it. Since it's still an outside-the-box way of being in a romantic relationship, it may not be immediately—or ever—embraced. The goal isn't to try to convince your partner that it's right for them, just that it's right for you.

"Come from a place of why it's important to you, the benefit to you. And then talk about the challenges, and ask and listen to your partner's perspective," she says.

For San Francisco Bay Area therapist and author Susan Pease Gadoua, it's more than just listening to their perspective; they need to understand their partner's attachment style, a theory founded in the 1950s by psychoanalyst John Bowlby that connects our bond with our primary caregivers—identified as secure, anxious-ambivalent, disorganized, or avoidant—to the way we approach relationships throughout our life. "The avoidant-attached person might be the one driving living apart, and they're going to be totally comfortable living apart, where a partner who's insecure, it might make them more insecure," she tells me.[155] "It may be something they, as a couple, may need to work out with a therapist. They may need to get guidance around that if they don't already know their styles."

"I'd want to know why" someone wants to live apart from their partner, psychologist Sherrie Sims Allen, who lived apart from her husband, Melvin, for five years and has a counseling practice with him, tells me. "When we work with couples, we work with their vision to create a vision statement for their lives, individually, especially if they're looking to get married and be in a relationship, and then have them join those visions together. Being on the same page before becoming a LAT relationship."[119]

Of course, she says, they'd counsel a cohabiting couple to do the same thing. But a LAT relationship requires more effort, she says, "because now you really need to turn toward each other to make sure the trust is there."

When you both agree on what living apart together means for each of you, you'll be better able to define what it will look like, and how your relationship will work when you're together and when you're not,[156] which we'll discuss in Chapter 5.

JEALOUSY AND JUDGMENT

Now that we've addressed our own potential ambivalence about choosing to be LAT, it's time to consider how others may view our choice. Because they will. While some longtime married people may think it sounds divine, many other people, married or not, may be confused, concerned, or dismissive, as we saw in Chapter 3. Or, as Sjogren observes, they may tell you your relationship isn't real. And that can take its toll.

"It wears you down: the murmurs that you must not be fully confident in what you have; the nagging worry that you're being indulgent or adolescent or just perverse," *The New York Times* columnist Frank Bruni wrote of his LAT relationship before he and his partner split.[157]

In his study of LAT couples, University of Málaga sociologist Luis Ayuso observes that if a couple is being pressured by family and friends to live together, they're more likely to cohabit or marry in the near future. "Despite the theories defending the importance of the individualization and privatization of the couple, the immediate cultural environment is pivotal."[158]

Although Abe and Elaine Romero, a couple in their second marriage who host the *Love Is in the Air* podcast, consider themselves in a long-distance relationship rather than LATs—she lives and works in California, he lives and works in Texas, and they hope to live together once his two children and hers are fully launched—they often hear annoying comments questioning their decision. Among them—what was their plan? How long were they going to do this living-apart thing, anyway?

"In a traditional relationship, you don't really ask . . . 'Oh, you're getting married now. What's your plan for the next five years?' It's an awkward thing to ask," Abe Romero says.[159]

Therapist Mazzei says if you've chosen to be in a live apart together relationship, you're likely on the way to having a more progressive or conscious way of viewing what romantic relationships can look like. If it's something you're considering, finding other like-minded people, whether through a Facebook group like Hyman's "Apartners" page or a Reddit subcommunity, can help combat potential feelings about being an outsider.

Either way, Mazzei says, it's important to set up healthy boundaries if you're choosing LAT or any other kind of romantic lifestyle that doesn't fit into societal norms.

"You get to choose who and when you spend time with. If you're surrounded by people who are judging you, not everyone has a need to know everything. Share it with people who are willing to listen," Mazzei says. "Who do you want in your inner circle? If you're feeling judged, can you process your own feelings about it? That's your responsibility. And if you're choosing LAT because you enjoy living alone, I think it's really wise to develop an ongoing self-love practice."

5 | RULES? WE DON'T NEED NO STINKIN' RULES

Several chapters into this book, one thing may be apparent—the people who choose to have a live apart together relationship treasure the freedom and flexibility it offers. So, it seems contrary that anyone desiring that would also choose to set up rules. And yet, in order for a LAT relationship to work, there must be some agreements in place. It's important to define your relationship—what living apart together means for each of you, and how you will make it work when you're together and when you're apart.

Do you agree on set days and times to be together, or do you prefer that things be more fluid? Whose place do you spend more time at, or is it fifty-fifty? How often do you communicate with each other, and with what technology? Do you have keys or access codes to each other's places and the ability to come and go as you please? Do you involve each other's children in activities?

How involved are you with each other's families and friends? Do you spend holidays together? Do you always take vacations together (and how do you share the expenses)? How far should you live from each other (if you are becoming LATs after living together or moving to be closer to each other)? Do you share travel costs if one person drives, flies, or takes other types of transportation more often than the other person to spend time together?

There are no guidelines to advise LAT couples on how to organize their relationship, no norms that they can turn to. That leaves each couple to decide for themselves what they'd like it to look like—a freeing decision for some and a challenge for others. In either event, it means communication, planning, setting boundaries, and then more communication.

"You have to be someone who can set boundaries," clinical psychologist Judye Hess tells me from her Berkeley, California, condo. And be "mature," she observes. What couples want to avoid is people-pleasing and any sense of codependency, especially feeling obligated to see your partner, perhaps because it's been a while or it's your scheduled day/night, but you'd rather be alone.[160]

That happens with all couples, whether they live together or not, but being LATs can accentuate the frustration and resentment.

Hess experienced it herself. When her romantic partner moved into a condo in her neighborhood a few years after they met in 1998, he started sleeping over every night, she says. She wasn't all that happy about it.

"It felt too routine, too set in stone," she says.

So, she addressed it from the start. After more than twenty-four years of living apart together, things have shifted several times.

"It's gone through so many iterations—he wants to come over;

do I want him to come over? If I ask him to come over, he'll usually come. I'm busier," she says.

"Now we have no rules; each day we decide what we're going to do that night, whether separate or alone," she says.

"We text during the day, not obsessively. He'll come over in the afternoon—it's a nice place to be. I give him my schedule every day, when I'm seeing my clients, and then he'll pop over," she tells me. Then he'll come over in the evening for an hour or so. They're a three-minute walk from each other, so it's an easy "commute," a situation not every LAT couple has.

One LAT couple in a second marriage I interviewed for *The New I Do: Reshaping Marriage for Skeptics, Realists and Rebels*—he lived and worked on the East Coast, and she lived and worked on the West Coast—had one major rule, that they never spent more than two weekends apart. In between, they made sure to talk on the phone every day and text several times a day. On Saturday mornings, they relied on FaceTime to connect.

CONNECTED WHEN APART

The goal is to stay connected when you're not together.

Some LATs call first thing in the morning or every night, or both. Some watch TV shows together while apart, or do Wordle, or crosswords, or have "date nights" by dressing up, setting the table with flowers and candles, and dining apart but together via a video chat. Some send selfies, naughty or nice.

There's no one perfect way to stay connected. It's a conversation you'll want to have—actually, it will be many conversations, as lots of things will change in your relationship over time.

Abe and Elaine Romero, a couple in their second marriage whom we met in Chapter 4, have set up rules to keep connected while she remains in California and he in Texas. They see each other every two to three weeks, she says on an episode of the

Real Relationship Talk podcast. "That became key. In order to make this work, we had to have a few trips on the books. It gave us a sense of hope."[161]

They also talk and text throughout the day—to the point that he believes their "communication and intimacy level far surpasses others," he says.

Taking advantage of the two-hour time differential, she typically sends a text before she goes to bed, so he'll see it first thing in the morning.

Both agree that a few things are essential—have a plan, connect throughout the day, and invest in yourself when you're apart by managing your own happiness, whether it's indulging in projects or having an active social life with family and friends, which not only alleviates any potential lonely feelings, but also goes far toward preventing an unhealthy neediness when you finally get to see each other.

Loneliness is something couples therapist Ili Rivera Walter, owner of CityCouples, an online therapy service, hears clients talk about most, especially if they have a traditional monogamous relationship.[162] "And not having comfort when you need it, immediately. You can have the comfort via FaceTime or via text, but it really is a totally different thing to go to your partner and get a hug when you need it," says Rivera Walter, who has been offering therapy for LAT couples since 2020, when she started seeing the lifestyle becoming a choice among her cohorts and eventually her clients.

Perhaps more than live-in couples, LAT couples need some guidance.

Good communication isn't necessarily intuitive. "So many partners, unless they have natural skills at this or were raised by very communicative families, in order to have that kind of openness, they need to learn new skills," she says. "It's not really an automatic thing to be able to ask for what you need, and asking your partner and being available for what they need. That is a really specific skill set that requires someone to get in touch with their own emotional triggers."

It's been fifteen years since Lise Stoessel and her husband, Emil, became LATs, and their relationship and arrangement have morphed. Still, they do have a structure in place, she tells me—three days a week together, although if things come up, as they sometimes do, plans may shift. Generally, they spend the weekends together and have dinner Tuesday nights at her house.[149]

"In choosing to live apart, my husband and I are really choosing to honor our individuality and honor each other's personal growth and honor each other's path and giving each other space to be who we are and who we want to become," she says. "It's so much less constrained."

E. A. Marconi and her late partner, Mason, had been dating for three years and living separately when, after a romantic trip to Venice, Italy, he asked her to live with him. Rather than move into his space, however, she took over the bottom unit of his duplex, and, after a few months, they put in a spiral staircase uniting the two units but still maintaining their separate spaces.

A year later, they wed, a second marriage for both.

"We never had any spoken rules," she tells me in an email. "We just knew one another well enough before I moved in with him to know that the only way our 'living independently together' would ever work was for us to keep our separate identities and independence. One thing I think was key was our level of respect for one another—we both trusted the fact that we would respect one another's space and give each other all the time they wanted in being alone or off doing their own thing."[163]

One thing to consider is how much access to your space your romantic partner has, and vice versa. Do they have a key or the access code to your space, and do you have theirs? As one study notes, "Having possession of a key means that one has free access to a room that would otherwise be closed (it is hardly a coincidence that a key has always had such symbolic significance)." As you can imagine, keys can sometimes be a sensitive issue in LAT relationships.[89]

In dating relationships, having a key to your romantic partner's place is often seen as a sign of commitment and trust, taking the relationship to another level. According to dating expert Susan Winter, "a key to your home or apartment allows them full access to your life. They are now in the center of your inner circle." It can make you feel more secure in your relationship—but also more vulnerable.[164]

Most LAT couples told me that they share keys or codes with their romantic partner, which is also seen as a way to build trust.[89] But, as with dating, having conversations and setting boundaries are essential. Can your partner come over whenever they want, or do they need to text or call first? Under what conditions could they come over unannounced?

YOURS, MINE, OR OURS?

Another consideration is time with family or friends or both. Do you spend time together as a couple with your partner's friends or extended family, or do you keep your social life outside your couplehood separate, or something in between?

In their study of LATs aged sixty to ninety years old in Sweden, Sofie Ghazanfareeon Karlsson and Klas Borell discovered that all the women they interviewed preferred to keep their friends and even family members, such as children and grandchildren, separate. They wanted to spend time with them on their own, using "their home to achieve a balance between intimacy and autonomy." This speaks to the fact that choosing to live apart is, as noted earlier in the book, often initiated by women as a way to create boundaries in a romantic relationship and to maintain their living space as "mine."[89]

As much as that could be a bonus, it could also prove stressful at times, such as during the holidays, especially if it means you're unable to be with your romantic partner because of family obligations.

Holidays are a tough time for many. It's when we're saturated with images of loving, joyful families opening presents around the Christmas tree or lighting the menorah, movies like *Home for the Holidays* and *I'll Be Home for Christmas*, and couples cozying up by a fire or kissing passionately at the stroke of midnight on New Year's Eve.

Even people who generally are satisfied with their life the way it is—whether they're happily partnered or happily single—can struggle during the holidays. Expectations are high. It's hard to fight the feeling that others are doing the holidays better (they likely aren't), or that they have more love, fun, and happiness this time of year than you do (they likely don't). And if you have children from previous relationships and you're living apart from your LAT partner, you may feel guilty that you're denying them that version of what many think a family "looks like."

It would be tempting to think that living under one roof with your romantic partner would give that experience to them and to you, that it would feel more like "home," perhaps like the one you grew up in—assuming that's a good memory (it isn't for many people). You may question your decision to be a LAT around this time of year, even if you appreciate all its upsides. As we explored in Chapter 4, ambivalence is baked into all romantic relationships, no matter their form. And it may be comforting to know that almost all couples wrestle with the whom to spend the holidays with dilemma.

If you know that you won't be able to be with your partner on a holiday, you may want to create some rules to capture that feeling of togetherness and home. Although she wasn't talking about LATs, parent educator Vicki Hoefle offers a great example of how to make that happen in her book *Parenting as Partners*. She tells a story of a mother's desire to greet her children with homemade, fresh-from-the-oven cookies after school, just like her mother did for her when she was young. It made her feel loved and cared for. But Hoefle wisely observes that it isn't really about the cookies; it's more about the feeling of unconditional love that she wants to re-create for her children. That's easy to understand. Except that feeling can come from creating experiences that have nothing to do with homemade, oven-fresh cookies.

"Many parents try to re-create with their children the positive experiences from their childhood but get stuck in trying to replicate the details rather than on capturing the feeling and meaning of the experience," Hoefle writes.[165]

This applies to adults in romantic relationships, too. Rather than trying to replicate the details, ask yourself what kind of structure you and your romantic partner can create to capture the feeling and meaning of the holidays when you're apart. Maybe you'll want more face time on Zoom, FaceTime, or some other technology. Lots of families celebrated the holidays as well as other celebratory occasions and milestone events via Zoom during the early days of the pandemic. It wasn't perfect, but it went far in offering a feeling of love, closeness, and togetherness.

Perhaps you'll agree to celebrate before or after the holiday, ideally as close to the actual holiday as possible, although it might be unexpectedly joyous to celebrate Christmas, Hanukkah, or Kwanzaa in July. Perhaps one of the rules you'll set up is that you must spend one winter holiday together a year. Or you may realize that spending Thanksgiving or New Year's Eve together isn't nearly as important to you as making sure you are together on each other's birthday, your anniversary, or Valentine's Day.

Again, the rules you set up as a couple should honor your goals, needs, and values both individually and as a couple.

Therapist Heather "Lulu" Mazzei says LAT couples aren't all that different from cohabiting couples, with one major difference—good communication is essential, as it can be more difficult to do. People who live together can have more eye contact on a regular basis, which is important to learn how to coregulate. She suggests understanding your partner's attachment type will go far in helping better communication.

"This is where a lot of people miss the mark, because they're not trying to understand the other person's communication preference," she tells me. "So, for people who are practicing LAT, communication may have to be even greater. If you're not living together, you don't have that kind of easy go-to."[122]

FIGHTING THE GOOD FIGHT
That applies to all sorts of communication, as well as setting up rules. And it applies to disagreements, because, yes, you're likely to have them.

Having an explicit agreement about how you'll handle disagreements is essential, says Rivera Walter. "Being able to say, 'Hey, I don't feel great about this. I need some time to process. I'll get back to you by X time.' Closing the loop and bringing your partner into, one, what you're feeling and, two, when you'll be available relationally for that conversation. That's really important."

That's helped Hess, who believes living apart from her partner has made disagreements easier. They make an appointment with each other to talk about an issue, which relieves some of the tension that often occurs in the moment when emotions may be high or one or the other of you is distracted.[160]

Again, it comes down to communication. "It's pretty generic," Hess says.

And rules, expectations, and agreements don't have to be written down, Rivera Walter shares.

"I do believe that the currency of romantic relationships is verbal contracts, whether they're spoken or unspoken. Even things we might not think of as a contract, if we agree, we are in an agreement, we are in a contract. As long as both people understand that," she says.

"It's not necessarily behavior that gets you into trouble in relationships, it's breaking an agreement—implied, explicit, or implicit. It's when you say you're not going to do something and you do it, that's what gets you into trouble. And that's everything from small things, like texting someone over their lunch break, to huge things like betrayal."

In her work with commuter couples and those in the military, who often spend months or years apart, clinical psychologist Wendy M. Troxel, senior behavioral and social scientist at the RAND Corporation, stresses the importance of a reunification period and readjusting couple dynamics and expectations when you're finally together.[166] When couples live apart, they're used to having a certain rhythm to their daily life. "Syncing up with someone else's rhythm, no matter how much you love them, can sometimes be challenging," she says. "It's joyful and wonderful and you really want to be with that person, but you're trying to resync each other's rhythms together."

And, she notes, it's OK to acknowledge that things may be easier when you're solo. Because they often are. It doesn't mean you love your partner any less if you admit that, and it's nothing to feel guilty about. They likely feel the same way.

6 | THAT'S SO MONEY

Money. It's the topic that couples regularly argue about, even if everything else in their relationship is going great.[167] In fact, money issues were cited as the third leading cause of divorce, behind basic incompatibility and infidelity, according to a survey from the Institute for Divorce Financial Analysts.[168] And the ways couples argue about money are "more intense and significant" than other issues argued about, according to studies, with bad behaviors expressed by both wives and husbands, but with husbands often becoming hostile, aggressive, threatening, and defensive.[169]

This sounds like something everyone might want to avoid.

Much of the research on couples' financial struggles is on married couples who live together (even if a spouse sometimes lives away for work or is in the military). There's scant research on how LAT couples handle money. In fact, one study noted that "the financial arrangements of couples living apart together are one area ripe for more exploration."[170]

That might matter more for researchers, but as noted earlier in the book, most couples don't structure their romantic partnership based on studies—they do what feels right for them.

Still, looking at the research that exists may highlight some financial issues couples hadn't anticipated.

Whether you're married or not and living together or not, research suggests that couples are most satisfied in their relationship when they share similar views and goals about their money, life goals, autonomy, and independence. In fact, that mattered more than having good communication[171]—something that seems contrary to what couples' therapists suggest.

So, it's distressing that a recent survey (by a financial services company, so take it with a grain of salt) indicates that a large percentage of people are financially incompatible with their romantic partner.[172] And another study, acknowledging that money in general is a taboo topic in our culture, finds that married couples don't discuss financial issues with each other as much as those who cohabit, and couples who are "non-cohabiting," which may or may not include LAT couples, discussed it the least.[173]

That could be because many people who choose to live apart together value financial independence. That's what a 2002 study of LATs aged sixty-five and older in Sweden discovered. In their desire to maintain their financial independence, most kept their finances separate, and few had joint savings or property.[174] But a 2012 study found that while couples "desired equality while attempting to maintain economic autonomy," the boundaries were fuzzy. Even if members of couples each took responsibility for their own money and didn't pool any of it, they often provided their romantic partner with an economic buffer and a certain amount of control, such as access to banking passwords and financial documents, and even some say on how the other's money was being used, as a way to express love and build trust.[175]

For other LAT couples, typically in their twenties and thirties, pooling money was seen as signaling a commitment to the relationship and its future.[176]

But couples are rarely true equal partners in financial resources and bargaining power, particularly in heterosexual couples, as women typically earn less than men and often drop in and out of the labor market for caregiving. So, it's not surprising that the perception of any sort of financial unfairness in a marriage increases the likelihood of divorce.[169] Plus, many couples still have gendered ideas when it comes to money, especially how it's controlled, managed, and allocated.

That can sometimes sneak into LAT relationships.

GENDERED EXPECTATIONS

In their exploration of fifty-four unmarried LAT couples in Belgium, sociologists Vicky Lyssens-Danneboom and Dimitri Mortelmans discovered some of the women allowed their partners to help financially with certain things—vacations and food—but most prioritized appearing fair and not wanting to feel indebted in any way to their romantic partner. If they perceived an imbalance, they made it up by doing (admittedly gendered) things for their partner, like cooking or cleaning.[177]

The men were somewhat ambivalent, believing sharing is a crucial aspect of being a couple, especially if they made more than their partner. Although they were supportive of their partners' "stubbornness"—an odd word choice, for sure—they still felt somewhat rejected in their ability to express their love and commitment to their partner. The researchers observe that for many of the men, being able to act as providers to their romantic partner, no matter their living arrangement, was important, and their ambivalent feelings suggest "that men continue to see bread-winning as a central part of their masculine identities. The importance men attach to breadwinning is often discussed in terms of the status and power it bestows."

Does that mean you should have a conversation with your male LAT partner (assuming you are heterosexual) about how money and being a provider may factor into how they define their masculinity? It couldn't hurt.

E. A. Marconi and her late husband, Mason, lived in Mason's duplex. He lived on the top unit, she lived on the bottom unit, and a spiral staircase they installed gave them easy access to both places.

Paying for her own space not only set up a financial boundary for Marconi, but also gave her a feeling of independence. Rather than have her husband pay for her unit in the duplex he'd bought before they met—a unit he earned rental income from before she moved in—she willingly contributed to the mortgage. "He didn't ask, I offered. I didn't want to give up my feeling of independence and I could afford to do so, so why not?" she tells me in an email.[163]

This, of course, raised eyebrows among family and friends. "People scoffed at this as in, 'How could he ask you to move in and then ask you to pay "rent"?'"

After about twenty years of living in separate units under the same roof, they made arrangements with an estate attorney "to make sure if I was left on my own, I would be 'taken care of.'"

Interestingly, in Lyssens-Danneboom and Mortelmans's study, the men were more willing to leave some of their property and financial assets to their LAT partner when they died; none of the women, however, were open to doing the same.[177]

Rachel Clark is in a LAT relationship of five years, but she and her partner, who each have children from previous relationships, have different attitudes about money. Keeping their finances separate has been a given since they became a couple.[178]

"My partner and I both earn enough to support a home and family on our own. If this weren't the case, I think we would buy a house together with room for all of us to spread out and maintain our independence," she says. That said, it wouldn't be easy. "Sharing space, bills, chores, etc., would put an enormous strain on the relationship, and I don't think we would be happy."

Still, Clark, a couples' counselor in Washington State, says talking about a financial future as a couple is important.

"We discuss investing in real estate together in the future. We support each other in getting out of debt and making good choices about saving for retirement, as we know that our future plans will depend on both of us being in a good place financially. We take turns buying dinner, paying for family activities, etc. We purchased a camper van together and share the costs," she says.

EQUAL OR EQUITABLE?

For married couples who live apart and have pooled resources, trust is essential. When you live together, it's easier to see what your spouse is spending money on, although, let's face it—hiding or lying about a financial decision is common even among couples who live together. According to a 2023 survey by *U.S. News & World Report*, more than a third of couples have been a victim of or committed financial infidelity, such as keeping purchases secret, hiding debts, lying about income, and even quietly depleting a joint savings account.[179] That's a heck of a lot of deception!

Whether you live together or apart, Debra A. Neiman, a certified financial planner and principal of Neiman & Associates Financial Services, says couples should have a full disclosure of their financial lives. That includes assets, income, credit scores, financial history, and debt.[25]

Often, there are financial disparities. "That's where things can get sticky," she says.

Splitting things fifty-fifty, like a pricey vacation or any type of joint expense, may seem fair, she says, but it's not if one person has significantly less income or fewer assets. You don't want your partner to be resentful, or to feel resentful yourself, so consider splitting those kinds of expenses proportionally, she suggests. It could also be a factor if transportation to see your LAT partner becomes a financial burden—something that could impact the relationship as you age together, as we'll discuss in Chapter 10.

Lise Stoessel and her husband, Emil, took their respective incomes into consideration when she moved out of the family home and into a place of her own about five miles away to salvage their marriage of nearly four decades. As a contractor, Emil makes more than Stoessel, a preschool teacher. They agreed that he was responsible for paying her mortgage, property taxes, and car insurance, and for their vacations, which are admittedly low-key. She pays all her other bills, such as groceries and utilities.[154]

It's not fifty-fifty, but it's proportional.

Therapist Judye Hess and her romantic partner of more than twenty-four years keep their money separate. When they travel, they generally split expenses evenly, although she admits she likes to stay in places somewhat pricier than his comfort level and so she pays the difference—a happy compromise.[160]

They now have what they call "The Tab," a running inventory of who owes whom what, versus emailing back and forth. "I hated getting those emails. I don't want to hear about money; I don't want to think about money, let's just live our lives," she says. "I just have to trust him. Money can be problematic when you have different values."

Their values are pretty aligned, she says, but Hess suggests couples communicate about how they think they've been handling money, and if things seem fair and balanced.

Many LAT couples who have experienced a divorce or other painful split have an acute awareness that romantic relationships often end and that the costs of such a breakup aren't just emotional—they're financial. That frequently helps drive their desire for financial independence. As one woman told researchers, if she ever got involved with anyone romantically again, she'd "want to make agreements on what to do with [joint purchases] in case it does go wrong or something."[72]

Neiman believes having a written agreement, drafted with an attorney, is important for LAT couples. No, it's not sexy, she admits. But it is smart, especially if you're a LAT couple who has been biding your time to move in together after your children from previous relationships are grown and flown, and especially if you're thinking about buying real estate together for a fresh start. Statistics show that second marriages are much more likely to end in divorce than first marriages.[180] And there's been no research to see if couples who lived apart and then married, whether they move in together or stay LATs, fare better.

"Buying property with someone is very emotional. And if that relationship should go south, what happens?" Neiman asks. Having a document in hand leaves little to no doubt. "I know it takes the romance out of it, but if something went south, it could get nasty. At least you have this document to refer to. Unlike married couples, where there's divorce court and formulas, it's calculated who gets what. At least you have this."

DO YOU PUT A RING ON IT?

Beyond buying property together, which you may or may not do, one thing to consider is whether you should put a ring on it if you're past a certain age. If you live in the United States, you may be better off financially if you don't.

In his 2022 paper "Preferencing Nonmarriage in Later Years," law professor Richard Kaplan, the Guy Raymond Jones Chair in Law at the University of Illinois, details how Social Security benefits and the potential need to move into a long-term care facility negatively impact the financial health of married couples.[181]

Social Security benefits are taxed at two thresholds—$25,000 for a single person and $32,000 for a married couple, and $34,000 for a single person and $44,000 for a married couple. Say you and your partner each earn $24,000, he writes. Neither of you would owe federal income tax on your Social Security benefit payments because your individual incomes are below the lower $25,000 threshold. But if you got married, now you'd have a combined income of $48,000—way beyond the $32,000 threshold, meaning a significant portion of your benefits would be taxed. It's even worse at the higher threshold.

That should give couples pause.

"The current income-tax structure pertaining to Social Security benefits makes nonmarriage the law's preferred status on this important and widely applicable issue," he writes.

When it comes to long-term-care facilities, which could cost in excess of a "frightfully expensive" $108,000 a year in the United States for a private room,[182] Kaplan reminds us that Medicare does not help pay for nursing home costs beyond short periods of posthospitalization recuperation; only Medicaid does—but that program only kicks in after you've spent almost all your assets and income, meaning you'll be pretty much broke. And if your or your spouse's income exceeds a minimum allowance as dictated by the state you live in, then some of that income might be required to help pay for the care facility. If you're not married, however, not one penny of your income would be touched.

Adding insult to injury, Medicaid can come after you to help defray your spouse's care-facility costs after they die. They can even come after your estate once *you* die—unless you're not married.

Some couples divorce later in life exactly to avoid these Medicaid problems, but as Kaplan tells me, Medicaid authorities will sometimes challenge recently divorced couples if they still live together.[183]

These are not just financial concerns for LAT couples, obviously, but they are certainly things to take into account if you're thinking of changing your unmarried LAT status. And while few of us want to end up in a care facility, sometimes circumstances are out of one's control.

That said, Kaplan brings up one benefit of tying the knot—if one of you plans to sell your house to either move in with your LAT partner or buy a new house together, you'll be able to claim a taxation gain of no more than $250,000 as a single person versus $500,000 for a married couple. But rather than wed—if you want to avoid the financial disasters of Social Security and nursing home care—Kaplan notes that all that has to happen is to make your partner a co-owner of your house (or vice versa). Problem solved.

These financial burdens may not be the same in the country you call home, but you would be wise to know what the rules actually are.

And as Gretchen Stangier, a financial planner in Oregon, points out, married LAT couples who live in different counties, states, or countries may face financial consequences if those places have different tax rates and requirements. Her suggestion—work with a tax pro.[184]

There are other financial perks and penalties of marrying or not.

If you live apart from your spouse in the United States and meet certain criteria, you may be able to file as head of household, which may lower your taxes. Who wouldn't welcome that?[185]

If you're not married, you might even be able to claim your romantic partner as a dependent on your federal income taxes if they meet certain Internal Revenue Service requirements. But here's the sticking point—that can only happen if your partner lives with you for at least a year and lists your home as their official residence.[186]

One thing research shows us is that when LAT couples end up marrying, it gives them a huge boost in life satisfaction, although researchers suggest that just may be the "legally binding character of marriage" as well as anticipating the actual wedding ceremony. And there's no way to put a price tag on that.[187]

Another thing to be clear about is inheritance.

Many romantic partners in their sixties and older choose to remain single and live apart together because they want to leave whatever property and assets they have to their children, who generally expect an inheritance (whether they deserve it or not). If you plan to leave your children an inheritance, tell them that and show them whatever paperwork you've put into play to protect them, such as a trust or life insurance or both. If you marry your LAT partner, consider getting a prenup or at the very least talk with an estate professional, experts suggest.[188]

Mostly, you will need to reassure your children, who can create havoc with their parents' new romances later in life, that they aren't forgotten, as you'll read in Chapter 8.

In a study of how divorced or widowed parents' romantic decisions are impacted by their adult children and stepchildren, researchers Jenny de Jong Gierveld and Eva-Maria Merz found that even LAT couples are suspect. One woman told them that her

LAT partner's adult daughter worried that she was "squandering" her father's money. The daughter treated her better once she saw that she continued to live in her own house and pay all her own expenses.[189]

The way to avoid all or at least most of the financial dilemmas detailed in this chapter is to start talking with your LAT partner and loved ones about money early and often, taboos be damned.

7 | THE FINE PRINT

I t would seem that there would be no need for the law to meddle in a romantic relationship where the people involved don't live under the same roof and don't spend all their time together. Any legal decisions a LAT couple makes shouldn't really be any different than the legal decisions couples who live together make.

That, unfortunately, isn't quite true.

The law hasn't always treated romantic partners who live apart from each other well. For example, before the US Congress passed the Bipartisan Safer Communities Act in 2022, the "boyfriend loophole," which prevented people convicted of domestic abuse from owning a gun, did not apply to couples who weren't married, didn't have a child together, and, most important, didn't live together. In the eyes of the law, unmarried LATs would likely be considered nothing more than dating partners.

Why does that matter? More than half of all intimate partner homicides have been committed by dating partners,[190] and according to Everytown for Gun Safety, the percentage of homicides committed by dating partners has been increasing for decades.[191] The new law, thankfully, now protects LAT couples.

Not so the United States' Fair Housing Act, which does not include marital status as a protected class. Moreover, in more than half of the states, marital status is entirely unprotected in housing—that is, unless there are stronger local laws, a landlord, property management company, or real estate agent can legally refuse to rent to someone simply for being single, even if they have a romantic partner who lives elsewhere.[192]

It's unknown how prevalent that is nowadays, but a 2007 study of housing rentals found that real estate agents overwhelmingly prefer to rent to a married couple over a cohabiting couple or singles, even if the applicants were similar in such things as age, hobbies, and careers.[193] So it's conceivable that an unmarried LAT couple could face housing discrimination if they are each seen as being single.

Another potential problem is unique to Americans who receive disability benefits, such as Supplemental Security Income (SSI). People with disabilities who marry can see a huge drop in or total elimination of their benefits under some conditions, even if they later get divorced. But an unmarried LAT couple could also have their benefits reduced or eliminated if the government considers them as "holding out"—a rather vague term meaning a romantic couple is presenting themselves as spouses. It typically applies to unmarried cohabitors but could possibly impact unmarried LATs if they publicly refer to each other as "husband" or "wife" or "my spouse," if they wear wedding rings, have a commitment ceremony, or engage in other public displays, as so many people do on social media platforms like Instagram, TikTok, and Facebook.

The government could look at the couple's social media pages and decide that they're "holding out," says Ayesha Elaine Lewis, staff attorney for the Disability Rights Education & Defense Fund.[194] It may not happen all that often, however, it's certainly something to be conscious of, she warns.

Other countries have their own ways of excluding LAT couples.

Portugal, for instance, passed the "shared economy" law in 2001, offering the same legal protections and benefits that married couples get to unmarried couples and any number of household companions regardless of their sexual orientation or relationship, but only if they live together. A few years later, the country passed a law recognizing same-sex marriage, which is hugely important. However, the law places numerous demands on spouses, including the need to cohabit, defined as "sharing bed, table, and house." In fact, cohabitation has been considered a marital duty in Portugal since 1910, and even today, married couples must list one address as the family home, even if they own or partially live in more than one house. So, if a married couple lives apart from each other, they could be considered to be violating the marriage contract and face whatever consequences result from that.[195]

Several Latin American countries have also recently changed their laws to give cohabiting couples the same rights as married couples, including such perks as inheritance (except Argentina and the Dominican Republic), alimony (except the Dominican Republic), and property rights (except Argentina, Chile, El Salvador, and Honduras). But notice that it's only for couples who live together, and who have lived together for at least two to five years, depending on the country,[196] and mostly for those who register their romantic partnership.[197] If you're a romantic couple who lives apart, you're out of luck.

Canada has similar restrictions. Kathie Brosemer lives next door to her LAT partner of more than six years in Sault Ste.

Marie, Canada. She's unable to have access to his medical benefits, however, because they don't live together, a situation she considers discriminatory.

"If we were living apart but married, his benefits would cover me. And if we were living together but unmarried, his benefits would cover me. In this case, they don't, just because he's in the house next door."[198]

So, you can see that LAT couples are often entangled with the law whether they want to be or not, and often not to their benefit.

CHALLENGES AND POSSIBILITIES

There is scant research on the legal treatment of LAT couples and their expectations. That's problematic because, as we've already seen, more people are becoming attracted to the lifestyle, and that's likely to continue, especially since marriage is losing favor across the globe and alternative arrangements, such as LAT and cohabitation, are growing. The more common such arrangements become, the more likely that legal issues might rear their heads.

That said, there are a few studies that point out challenges and potential fixes moving forward.

As Cynthia Grant Bowman notes in her 2020 book *Living Apart Together: Legal Protections for a New Form of Family*, things like health care, welfare benefits, and pensions shouldn't be based on marital status, as they are in the United States, but on someone's status as an individual. This, she writes, would allow each of us to choose the kind of living arrangement we prefer without fear of any economic repercussions.[199]

She is not the first legal scholar to advocate for those changes.[200] That, however, does not seem to be happening anytime soon. Still, in her research on LATs, Bowman discovered that many engage in mutual caregiving and sometimes share finances or property. And because society benefits from that caregiving, family law should encourage and support people's caregiving regardless of whether they live together or not. So, the Cornell Law School law professor lists a few legal changes that would provide some protections for those in LAT relationships.

She suggests a system of registration of LAT partnerships should couples want to formalize their romantic relationship. For those who choose not to register, legal rights should be available anyway once a LAT relationship has lasted for more than five years, unless they are what she considers "young" or "dating" LATs, usually between the ages of eighteen and twenty-four, unless they are registered.[201]

Researchers Simon Duncan, Miranda Phillips, Sasha Roseneil, Julia Carter, and Mariya Stoilova advocate for similar protections in their 2011 research briefing, such as offering legal recognition to LAT couples who wish to "opt-in."[202]

While Bowman doesn't see a need for tax law to treat LAT couples as one economic unit while they are alive, "designation as the primary beneficiary of a will or pension is in the nature of an intentional provision for postmortem support analogous to a contract and also a form of postmortem caretaking, and thus such treatment appears just."[199]

Lastly, Bowman states that family law should not punish or interfere with a LAT lifestyle in any way. This sometimes occurs after divorce, where alimony is ended if the former spouse—typically the wife, as women make up the majority of those receiving alimony, although more men are making inroads—is thought to be cohabiting, a rule that sometimes ensnares LATs. Indeed, there are statues in twelve states—Arkansas, Illinois, Louisiana, Maine, North Carolina, Ohio, Pennsylvania, and Texas among them—that automatically cut off alimony once a couple cohabits, a situation that could also impact LATs, she notes.[203] This is information you'd want to know if you happen to live in one of those states, so you'll need to do your research.

Bowman notes the obvious gendered injustice of such a rule: "The fact that termination is triggered in most cases only by a relationship involving sex indicates that the rule functions to penalize the choices of relationship made by women who receive alimony and to police their sexuality more generally."[204]

In 2020, a Canadian LAT couple made waves when the top Ontario court ruled that wealthy businessman Michael Latner must pay more than $50,000 a month in spousal support for ten years to Lisa Climans, his long-term romantic partner, even though the Toronto couple lived in separate houses, had separate bank accounts, and had no children together.[205] They did, however, act like a committed romantic couple, publicly and privately, with Latner giving Climans thousands of dollars every month, a credit card, expensive gifts, and even paying off her mortgage.

Under Ontario law, unmarried couples are considered common-law spouses if they have cohabited continuously for at least three years. But the Appeal Court determined that "cohabiting" doesn't necessarily mean living in the same house.

"There are many cases in which courts have found cohabitation where the parties stayed together only intermittently," the court wrote.

Meaning that unmarried LAT couples can possibly be considered spouses and thus may need to provide or be eligible to receive financial support if the relationship ends—at least in Canada.

How did that happen? Canadian courts look at certain conditions to consider a couple cohabiting, including:[206]

- Shelter (the living arrangements of the couple)
- Sexual and personal behavior (were the couple in a sexual relationship, how often did they communicate and in what ways, did they give each other gifts, etc.?)

- Services (did the couple prepare meals for each other, wash or mend clothes, shop with or for each other, help maintain each other's living spaces, etc.?)
- Social (did the couple do activities together, have relationships with each other's family and friends?)
- Societal (was the couple understood to be in a committed relationship?)
- Financial (arrangement of finances, who purchased food, clothing, shelter, recreation, etc.)
- Children (what was the attitude and conduct of the couple concerning children?)

If the couple has a child together, the courts will also look to see if they have been "cohabiting in a relationship of some permanence"—generally meaning they've been together for a while in a well-established relationship of some sort—and one of them could collect spousal support.

In 2012 Professor Simon Duncan asked LAT couples in Britain, where about ten percent of couples identified as living apart together at the time, about their thoughts on legal rights for LAT couples, what they consider their responsibilities to their partner, and their care and everyday couple practices and understandings.[207]

About a third—with a median age of forty-four—didn't think LAT couples should have legal rights. As odd as that might seem, they were the ones who most embraced the autonomy of living apart together and didn't want to repeat the emotionally and financially exhausting separations of previous romantic relationships. They also were protective of keeping their identities, as well their finances and property, separate. Of all the people Duncan surveyed, they had been in their LAT relationship the longest and expected to continue living apart together.

The others he surveyed fell into two groups: those who believed legal rights might be appropriate depending on circumstances, such as length of the relationship, and those who believed legal rights should be extended to LATs, most of whom planned to live together or marry at some point and wanted to be able to have their partner have access to their finances, pensions, or property.

His findings are similar to a 2013 study of fifty-four individuals in a LAT relationship in Belgium.[208] While many didn't expect to have marriage-like legal rights, some thought that they should have the same family-based benefits as those given to cohabiting or married couples. Unmarried cohabitants in Belgium who are registered—considered "legal cohabitation"—have slowly been given legal rights similar to those given to married couples, such as paid leave to care for a sick partner, as well as inheritance taxes, gift taxes, and disability and unemployment insurance. Even unregistered cohabiters enjoy some perks similar to married couples.

Not LATs, however. There's no legal protection if the relationship ends, they're not considered next of kin, they're not eligible for paid leave to care, or to attend their LAT partner's funeral or to grieve, and they're not entitled to any of their LAT partner's property and assets unless there's a will. In addition, the researchers note, "if LAT partners inherit by will or if they endow each other, they are treated as complete strangers and are liable to significantly higher taxes than are married or cohabiting couples."

When asked about their current legal position, those surveyed were caught by surprise—"I've never really thought of that"—but assumed they wouldn't be entitled to anything, although they understood how important it is to make legal arrangements, even if they neglected to do so.

Still, many noted that because they don't share a household, they are not seen as a "real" couple, a situation they found to be fundamentally unfair (and that we explored in Chapter 4). To address that, many believe legislators, and public and private institutions, should grant intimate partners rights and benefits on the basis of their existing bond and not on whether they share a household or not.

As Duncan writes, "many LAT partners considered their relationships to be joint relational projects where they felt highly connected and committed to their partner, and some (if not all) performed significant levels of care, support, household labour and childcare," raising the question many legal scholars have asked—why do we continue to privilege only those who marry?

That, of course, is beyond the scope of this book. That said, legal experts do have some thoughts about what LAT couples may want to consider.

PLANNING WITH INTENTION

Diana Adams, executive director and president of Chosen Family Law Center in New York City and an expert and leader in support of LGBTQ+ and polyamorous families and nontraditional family structures, suggests that LATs be open and honest about their intentions and how they want their relationship to look.[209]

If couples are coming up with a private contract, Adams, who uses the pronouns *they* and *them*, says it's important to get it legally notarized and have an attorney review it to make sure that it is valid. That isn't as important for what they call an emotional contract, when couples set up mutually agreed-upon behavioral rules about what's OK and what's not, and how they want the relationship to function.

"Anything that's going to be related to custody of children or money, or the ability to visit each other in the hospital, that's when you're in a three-way agreement with the state and you need to make sure that you have a lawyer review that and it's actually valid," they tell me. "You need to make sure it's relatable to the world."

Bowman, too, is a fan of contracts between LAT couples and believes contracts that address such things as property and financial issues should be recognized and enforced, as they are in many states for cohabiting couples.[210]

But if LAT couples want their partner to get all or a share of their estate, a will is essential. "They really have no claim at all if you don't make a will," Bowman tells me.[211] Despite that, just forty-six percent of Americans have a will.[212] In her research of LAT couples in the US, only nineteen percent of those who responded had a will providing for their partner; those who did have a will were predominately aged forty-five to fifty-five.[213]

Same with a health care power of attorney, she says. Having a health care power of attorney matters even if you have adult children, especially if they don't live near you, and if your LAT partner is the person you trust with your health care decisions. Otherwise, she says, your partner "may not even have access to you" in health care situations and emergencies.

And because of America's wonky alimony laws, as noted above, Bowman suggests LAT couples keep their finances separate. That isn't always the case with couples who live apart, she notes. "Our alimony laws are wrong, I think, but in many states a husband could say you're cohabiting and that's a reason to terminate alimony. And that could turn out really leaving a lot of women in bad financial shape," she tells me.[211] Again, a contract detailing each of your financial and independence could help avoid such a situation.

Sometimes LAT couples weigh whether to marry or not. Adams notes that the decision has consequences both good and bad, such as assessing the tax penalties if you're leaving a certain amount of money or property to your LAT partner if you don't marry, or if you're a widow and you'd lose your former spouse's pension if you do. "Marriage can be used as a legal and financial tool. It's important for people to have that conversation, that marriage is not just about romance, it's about, 'Is this particular legal tool right for our partnership?'" they say.

Ultimately, it's going to involve conversations, not just one but many throughout the relationship as things change.

"Whether or not you create legal agreements, any kind of relationship in which you are really emotionally invested, it makes sense to have a conversation about what your intentions are. Are we intending to be monogamous and not making that an assumption; if not, what are our sexual health policies? Are we intending to intertwine our finances or not? Are we wanting to spend most of our vacations and holidays together or are we not? What does freedom and independence mean to you and how can I support that?" Bowman says.

"The more we can get off the relationship escalator and make assumptions about the way relationships are 'supposed to look,' and realize we can design them ourselves, the better. And that means just having these open conversations."

8 | WHAT ABOUT THE KIDS?

Lisa Lubin never wanted to have children or even get married. So, when she and her partner got together thirteen years ago—they had known each other since high school and reunited in their late thirties—she saw a problem. His kids were still young, just one and five, and she didn't want to be another mom to them. She was living happily in Chicago, and he lived in New Jersey, but whenever she'd visit him, it was tense.

"He couldn't balance being there for me, being there for them," she tells me.[214] After trying to make that work for a few years— "I was never happy in his space"—they thought they weren't compatible. So, they broke up.

Except they still really loved each other. Then, a lightning bolt hit: *We don't have to live together*, she thought. It was a complete mind shift. They got back together after about a year and a half but continued to live apart, which allowed him to focus on his children when they were with him and on her when he stayed with her or when she stayed with him during the week his kids were with their mom.

During the COVID-19 pandemic, Lubin decided to leave Chicago and buy a house in Pennsylvania to switch up her life a bit and to be closer to her partner. They even cohabited for a year until she found a house. That time together confirmed that they were not good partners under one roof.

Now that his children are older, Lubin has a bigger presence in their lives. "I don't necessarily parent them. I couldn't make myself part of his family; it's just organic. Literally, I'm like their stepmom, and every stepparent has different degrees of involvement," she says. "They know me as his partner, and I love them and care about them, and I think they're used to it, how our relationship is."

Lubin and her partner are one of many couples who decide to live apart in part because of the children one or both have from previous relationships. As we saw in Chapter 2, attempting to combine families in one household can be challenging for some couples, especially if a child is neurodiverse or has special needs. So, living apart together is a way for couples to put the children's needs first while still honoring the couplehood.

Living apart together allows romantic partners to nurture their relationship—"to get to know and connect with your partner without the 'noise' of dealing with kids in the mix"—while also focusing on their children in their time apart, says Ann Turner, a couples and family therapist who works with stepfamilies.[215]

That works for Lauren Apfel, a mother of four, and her girlfriend, who has one child. It allows them to focus on their relationship when they're together while avoiding a lot of the tension stepsiblings often experience. It also sidesteps dealing with differing parenting styles.

"Living apart allows us to uphold the distinct parenting values we each champion and to not have to compromise them in the name of treating everybody the same," writes Apfel, cofounder and executive editor of *Motherwell*.[216]

Still, even if you don't live together, if you're romantically involved with someone and you or they or both of you have minor children at home (or even adult children who have moved out), some conversations are going to have to happen, and some agreements are going to have to be made. Do we discipline each other's children, and, if so, when, and how? How often do we gather as a family? Do we take vacations together? Do we spend holidays together? Do our children spend time alone with our romantic partner when we're unavailable? Do we share any childcare costs? What if we disagree on parenting styles? How often do we interact with our romantic partner's children's other parent(s), if at all? How can we feel like a family if we're not living together?

These conversations will be different than the ones you'll have if you are raising your own child or children while living apart from their other parent, which we'll discuss later in this chapter, since it's more common that LAT parents with children living at home are raising children from previous romantic relationships.

If you have children from previous relationships and are living as LATs with your current romantic partner, therapist Heather "Lulu" Mazzei suggests couples take cues from the polyamory community—not sexual cues, obviously, but the intentional conversations that offer a sense of family, albeit in a different form.[122]

"It goes back to being really intentional. Discussing when would we like to meet each other's children, under what context, how do we bring this up to our children so it's not shoving it in their faces? It takes a lot of thoughtfulness," she says.

One thing LAT couples with children from previous relationships have over stepfamilies living under the same roof is that they give their children space to get used to their new parent figure and any stepsiblings so they can form a relationship in their own way and in their own time.

"[K]ids are hard-wired to connect to their parents. They often are not very interested . . . in having a stepparent come in and disrupt their lives," notes Patricia Papernow, a psychologist and author of three books on stepparenting. "The research is very clear: kids are not ready for a stepparent's discipline until or unless that stepparent has formed a caring, trusting relationship with his or her stepchild."[217]

It doesn't always go as easily as hoped for.

There aren't many studies about the role children and stepchildren might play in influencing how their parents approach a new romantic relationship, whether they choose to marry, meld households, or become LATs. Researchers acknowledge that this lack of knowledge is unfortunate, as once you become a parent, you're a parent for life and children's well-being matters, even if your children are adults and no longer living at home. A new romantic relationship may jeopardize the parent-child relationship or limit contact with adult children or grandchildren. Which, as we've already seen, is in part why many parents with minor children from previous relationships prefer to live apart from a new romantic partner.

One Swedish study indicated that while having children increases the likelihood that parents won't move in with a new partner, it doesn't seem to hinder parents from living apart from a new partner.[218]

A study of twenty-five middle-aged divorced and widowed people in the Netherlands also indicated that children who lived at home played a huge role in preventing their parents from living with a new partner. However, they sometimes created obstacles for LAT couples nonetheless, forcing them to arrange their time together only when their children were not around, such as on the days or nights when their children were with the other parent.[189]

The same study found that even some adult children who no longer lived at home still reacted poorly to a new partner, sometimes reducing the number of times they visited their parents, not allowing their children to visit their grandparent, or refusing to create any sort of bond with the new partner. We'll see how that could create complications later in life for LATs in Chapter 10.

All of which makes your children's thoughts and feelings about a new LAT romantic partner an essential part of your conversations.

Although Lise Stoessel's stepdaughters, Lisi and Julie, were already grown and out of the house and her youngest, Susanah, was in college when she and her husband decided to become LATs, it's clear that all three daughters felt the stresses and unhappiness of their parents' marriage, what Lisi describes in Stoessel's book *Living Happily Ever After—Separately* as a complicated and sometimes unpleasant past.[219]

The stories they shared in the book reveal why they have come to believe that the LAT arrangement was not only good for their parents, but also for their entire family.

The stepmother Julie knew as a child was often in bad moods and critical, albeit caring, she observes. "I have gone from having a stepmother I looked up to but was often fearful of, to having someone whom I can trust not only to be there when I need her, but also to respect me as I respect her."[220]

Susanah observes that after her mother moved out, she felt a shift in the family. Their parents' reconfigured marriage allowed each member of the family to "shrug off layers of defensiveness and self-preservation" and become more sensitive and tuned in to each other, she writes.[221]

Given how tense Stoessel's marriage was, would she have

become LATs sooner? When I asked Stoessel that, she said she was unsure—"It's a complicated answer"—but probably not. Mostly because when they wed, they moved her husband's two elementary-school-age daughters from his previous marriage away from their mother. That's what made their situation difficult, prompting anxieties about abandonment. "With these sort of fraught dynamics, it would have been much more painful if we split up sooner for them."[149]

If you're a stepfamily in a similar situation and thinking about transitioning from a live-in situation to a live apart together arrangement, feelings of abandonment might be something to consider.

But what if you and your romantic partner don't have children from previous relationships, or you do but would like to have a child together? Can you live apart from the other parent of your child? We already briefly acknowledged in Chapter 3 that, yes, you can. Do you want to? And if you decide that you do, how can you do it well?

CHALLENGING NORMS

When their children were just one and three years old, famed British-Turkish novelist Elif Shafak decided to live apart from her husband, Turkish journalist Eyüp Can Sağlık—she in London and he in Turkey, a distance of some fifteen hundred miles.

"The children are happy here, they receive a good education, are learning to be world citizens, and are somehow content with having two homes in two cities," she shared in 2017, four years after her bold move.[222]

She acknowledged that perhaps it works because the children were so young when their parents became LATs, so they didn't know much different. They might have resented it if they were teens, she said, and they still might one day.

Nevertheless, she believes "[e]ach couple needs to discover what works best for them and for their children, and when that doesn't work any longer, they need to find another way, sometimes at the expense of challenging the society's established norms."

How can taking children away from one parent for so long be good for them, you might be asking. It's a question many would-be LATs or LATs who are considering having children ask. How can parents raise a child if they're not living under the same roof? Will it harm the child? Will they feel equally connected to both parents?

Unfortunately, there is hardly any research on the impact on children growing up with LAT parents. That said, it's not as if there aren't any models to turn to.

As weird as it may seem, many divorced parents do it all the time—they raise their children together while living apart. Perhaps not fifteen hundred miles apart—many divorce arrangements don't allow a parent to move their children far from the other parent. Still, as Shafak says, couples often need to get creative to discover what works best for them and for their children, and what's best may change over time.

When journalist Brandie Weikle and Derek DeCloet's twelve-year marriage ended in divorce in 2017, they made a brave choice that might seem unusual to many formerly married couples— DeCloet left the family house in Toronto and moved into the house next door with his new wife. The goal was to create a welcoming place for the former couple's two young boys that was close to their first home.

It seemed to work well. "I guess it's a new way of doing it. It's normal to us," their son Cameron, then thirteen, said at the time.[223]

Not every divorced couple is as friendly and cooperative as Weikle and DeCloet, or as actor and Goop founder Gwyneth Paltrow, who famously consciously uncoupled in 2014 from

Coldplay front man Chris Martin, with whom she shares two children. The two have continued to live near each other, even when she married again in 2018. The reason? To put their children first.

"[W]e thought if we could maintain the family even though we're changing the shape of it, it would be, that would be our ideal scene and so, that's what we're trying to do," she said in 2015.[224]

The huge and important difference between LAT parents and divorced parents, of course, is that presumably there is love, friendship, commitment, shared goals, and intimacy between the LAT parents and not the friction and anger many divorced parents experience, in addition to parental warmth and love expressed toward their children. Study after study has shown that parental conflict and how they deal with it is what's most harmful to children, and conflict occurs in both divorced and intact families.[225]

If living apart together reduces or removes conflict and makes a couple happy, then their relationship will benefit and so will their children. As Susan Golombok, professor emerita of family research and former director of the Centre for Family Research as the University of Cambridge, observes, "there is growing evidence that the more favorable outcomes for children of happily married parents do not simply result from the absence of serious conflict, but, instead, are more directly associated with positive aspects of the relationship, such as the way in which parents communicate with each other and show each other affection."[224]

That can happen even if parents don't live together. Researchers found that Swedish children who live with both parents after separation have the same self-esteem and parental support as children living in a nuclear family.[227]

Children will also benefit by having parents who understand exactly what their children need from them. Children have one essential need—to feel safe and secure, child development expert

Nancy Carlsson-Paige tells me. And they can feel safe and secure no matter what their family form looks like. "Living apart together is just one other way to arrange a living situation. I don't think it makes or breaks the children's sense of security and well-being. I don't think the arrangement is what's very important. What's important is meeting the needs that children have."[228]

And doing it in a way that they can make sense of developmentally. Younger children need things to be explained simply, such as which parent's home they're going to and when. And then it's on the parents to stick to the schedule. If you're helping your young child learn time and you tell them that their other parent is coming over at 6 p.m., "that other parent has to show up. They can't come at eight o'clock," Carlsson-Paige says.

Older children don't necessarily need that level of specificity. That said, parents will still need to stick to what's been agreed to. If there's a change in the schedule, they, too, need to be told in a way they understand.

"We don't ever want to undermine their sense of agency, autonomy, and their sense of security—'I know I can count on these people,'" she says. "Doing this in a way that provides them with the same sense of security they would have if everybody was under the same roof, and they could see them, is the only issue the adults in the situation should have in the forefront of their mind."

Parents in platonic parenting partnerships, a growing concept in which people who are not romantic partners agree to raise a child together, also make it work. The United Kingdom recently ruled that two people, one of whom is gay, in a long-standing platonic marriage who live in separate homes are recognized as the platonic parents of their child, born by a surrogate, who splits time with each parent. Co-living is not a requirement to grant parenting rights in the UK.[229]

Rachel Hope, author of *Family by Choice: Platonic Partnered*

Parenting, has two children with two different coparents. Hope and her first child's father, with whom she was not romantically involved, lived together when their baby was born. That was challenging, she says, and so they eventually decided to live next door to each other.[230]

When Hope wanted another child, but her platonic partner didn't, she turned to a longtime friend, and they are now platonic parents of a girl. They, too, lived together at first, but he now lives a short walk away and has a room of his own in Hope's house.

Hope was very intentional in choosing who would father her children based on shared values and a strong commitment to having an intact family—no matter the living arrangement. As she says, "Any relationship/family is only as good as the people in it."

FROM ONE ROOF TO TWO

So, if divorced parents and platonic parents can change the shape of their family and still parent their children, all couples—married or not—can change the shape of their family, too. Of course, there are considerations, especially if you started off living under one roof and are considering living in different spaces.

Depending upon their age, your child may be angry, unhappy, or both. They may also see you as being selfish (you may worry about that as well). Your commitment to the family may be questioned. You may find yourself wondering that, too, as well as feeling pangs of guilt, as discussed in Chapter 4. And you may find that your LAT arrangement may be blamed for anything and everything that seems problematic in your child's life—from getting a C-minus on a spelling test to the marijuana found stashed in your teen's drawer.

Therapist and *The New I Do* coauthor Susan Pease Gadoua works with couples on the verge of divorce by helping them remove the romantic and sexual aspect of their union and instead focus on coparenting in a loving and respectful way—what she calls a parenting marriage. She suggests parents know the attachment needs of their children before they tell them they're changing the family form.[155]

Finding the right language to explain it to them and reassuring them of your love for them and for their other parent is essential. Just as important is your tone of voice, she says.

"No big buildup, just like, 'Hey, we just want to let you guys know that we have decided that we want to have separate houses and that means you guys get two rooms, isn't that cool, and you're going to go back and forth between the two houses and if you have any questions let us know.' Present it in a 'this is going to happen, it's no big deal' kind of tone," she says. "Kids are taking their cues from adults about how they should feel. If the parents are totally cool with it, it's more likely they'll be."

It's a similar approach to helping your children deal with other kids' questions or judgments about your outside-the-box living situation, whether LAT is a new arrangement or whether they never experienced their parents living together.

"If a kid comes to a parent and says, 'I'm getting really bullied at school because you guys don't live together,' I would work with the parents to help the kid to feel better about the choice, to not feel apologetic about the choice, letting them know nobody's doing anything wrong here and in fact, we're doing it because we're able to and that's a really cool thing," she says. "And telling kids that people aren't going to always understand, it's not the norm at this point."

During the 2008–2009 recession, a lot of families Gadoua was working with were forced to be creative when an unemployed parent had to take a new job far away from the family. So parents had to present the new situation matter-of-factly to their children—"we don't really have a choice."

WHAT ABOUT THE KIDS?

It isn't much different for parents who are choosing to live apart. It's also a matter-of-fact conversation and one that can be presented as a positive: "We're so lucky to live apart. We get along so much better," she says.

Plus, she notes, children nowadays are growing up in a time of lots of diversity in family form. They're more likely to know other children who are being raised by a single parent by choice, two mothers or fathers, stepparents, divorced parents, grandparents, cohabiting parents, unmarried parents, or in multigenerational homes than those who are being raised by what many consider a traditional nuclear family—a mom and dad who are still married and live together. According to the Pew Research Center, Americans increasingly say these new family forms don't make a difference, and many believe it's actually a good thing.[231]

"Kids coming up now . . . are not bound by the same constrictions we had growing up," Gadoua, a baby boomer, says. "They're much more fluid with everything, from gender to family. It's going to be less of a thing."

Still, children need to know what's going on and why.

Young children don't think like adults, Carlsson-Paige says. "They don't think abstractly. They think much more in concrete terms. . . . It's amazing how helpful it is and how satisfied they are with a simple explanation when they're younger."

It could be as simple as saying, "Daddy Alan likes to get up early and Daddy Robert likes to stay up late, so it's so much easier if we have our separate houses and you get to live in both."

Older children tend to ask more questions and start to probe, Carlsson-Paige says. This requires parents to become what she calls deep listeners. "It's a matter of listening to the question they have and trying to make sense of what the question is. . . . What is it that this child needs in this conversation?"

Family by Design, a website for would-be platonic parents,

suggests coparents tell their child that there are many types of families; if your child asks why they can't have a live-at-home mom or dad like their friends have, "you can explain how your family has just as much love, and just as much value, in its special structure as that of a family with a different structure."[232]

Becoming a parent is about the biggest change in a person's life, one that's lifelong, affecting how we see ourselves and how others see us, and with all the legal, financial, physical, and emotional realities that come along with having a child. Few people are truly prepared for that. Yet, LAT parents can take some cues from platonic parents.

There are structures that can be set up to have your child's life continue as normal, or as close to what they've come to know as normal, in two homes, perhaps having duplicates of their favorite clothes or toys so there's less to pack up as they move back and forth. Creating a calendar or a schedule of when they'll be at one place or the other, or when the other parent is coming to visit, may help. If the children spend more time at one parent's house, setting aside specific days and times when the other parent can chat with them on the phone, FaceTime, Skype, or Zoom, is important, too, given most children's jam-packed school and extracurricular schedules. In between, you can text. The goal is to maintain a meaningful connection with your child and have everyone feel that you're one family, even if you're in separate spaces.

Carlsson-Paige is a fan of having some sort of ritual or a transition object such as a lovey (like a stuffed animal) or a blanket to help children switch between homes. "Rituals are important to kids at all ages. Teens may pooh-pooh it, but they probably really like it. Rituals are a wonderful way to mark the transition, especially for younger kids," she says.

And parents can be creative about it. "It doesn't matter what it is—it helps the kids concretize the transition. Transitions are hard for all of us. Make it more meaningful, more understandable."

Although commuter relationships are different from LAT relationships, LAT parents can also learn from how commuter parents make it work. In their 2007 report "Miles That Bind: Commuter Marriage and Family Strengths," Richard Glotzer, director of the School of Family and Consumer Sciences at the University of Akron in Ohio, and Anne Cairns Federlein, former president of Kentucky Wesleyan College, note that parents who are considering living apart should sit down and detail their strengths and weaknesses and whatever pressures they believe they may confront. It's worth the time and money for couples to work with a counselor or therapist to gain an informed, objective assessment of their goals, potential stresses and problems, and, particularly important, unspoken issues, they say.[233]

"Families tend to underestimate the rough ride they are designing for themselves and its potential long-term consequences. Minor issues may become major ones under unforeseen circumstances and may threaten family relationships and stability, as well as family goals," they write.

At the minimum, they say, is a "stable egalitarian relationship with open family-wide communication and agreement on the goals and parameters" of their LAT arrangement. Also essential is flexibility in family roles, being efficient at planning and time use, learning to live with ambiguity, and being reliable.

At the heart of a decision to parent as LATs, they say, is to make it a child-centered arrangement. There are many ways to be both a thoughtful and collaborative romantic partner and a parent, they observe. It starts with a commitment to one's family as well as love for one's children and concern for their well-being and future.

And that may mean children don't bounce back and forth between your two separate homes.

Author Judith Newman and her late husband, John Snowdon, raised their two boys together despite never living under one roof until he became ill, and caretaking was essential. Their boys didn't question it much, she writes, because Snowdon ate dinner with them and tucked them into bed nightly and stayed over about three nights a week. Their children even enjoyed talking about their "uptown and downtown houses."[234]

Was it hard sometimes? Yes, she admits, especially when the kids were sick and she really wanted help. And yet I often felt the same way when I was living under the same roof with my then husband and one or both of our boys had a fever or started puking and their dad was away on business. Because, for some reason, children almost always get sick when one parent is gone.

In other words, worrying about the few times you may feel overwhelmed being the primary parent should not heavily influence your decision on whether to be LAT parents or not.

For Canadian couple Sharry Aiken and Rudhramoorthy Cheran, living apart has been essential for their careers in academia. She's associate dean of graduate studies and research, and associate professor, in the law department at Queen's University in Kingston, Ontario, and he's associate professor in the department of sociology, anthropology, and criminology at the University of Windsor in Windsor, Ontario—a few hundred miles away. They bought a house in Toronto, which they've traveled to and from while raising their now-teen twins together.

They arranged their lives so that one of them is always with their children at their Toronto home and they can spend their weekends together as a family. They also relied on an on-call sitter for emergencies.[235]

In her 2019 book *Commuter Spouses: New Families in a Changing World*, sociologist Danielle J. Lindemann found that while some of the couples she interviewed were concerned that having a parent be absent for so long could negatively impact their children, others told them that their children greatly benefited from the arrangement, not only learning how to be independent, but also how to "take care of themselves"[236]—traits that parenting experts such as Dr. Dana Suskind, author of *Parent Nation: Unlocking Every Child's Potential, Fulfilling Society's Promise*, and psychologist Madeline Levine, author of *Ready or Not: Preparing Our Kids to Thrive in an Uncertain World*, say children need to face the challenges ahead.

All these parents are making conscious, deliberate, and thoughtful decisions on how to best give their children what they need as well as acknowledging their own needs.

MAKING A PLAN

Talking to a therapist could help LAT parents address similar issues. So could creating a parenting plan, something Gadoua and I suggest in *The New I Do: Reshaping Marriage for Skeptics, Realists and Rebels*, as well as author Vicki Hoefle, a retired parenting coach, in her 2017 book *Parenting as Partners: How to Launch Your Kids Without Ejecting Your Spouse*.

"It's natural that you and your partner would have different ideas on how to raise kids. You undoubtedly have different ideas about where to vacation, how to spend your leisure time, how many social invitations to accept in the course of a month, how to decorate your home, how important exercise is to a healthy life, how much to put in your retirement account, what kind of car to buy, and so on. Why do we think that a short conversation about raising another human being is all that's required of us? And why doesn't it occur to us that we are going to have to spend a significant amount of time collaborating with our spouses if we want to co-parent successfully?" she observes.[237]

Creating a plan about such things as parenting philosophies, discipline, schooling, religion, vaccinations, bedtime rules, etc., will help each parent know that they're on the same page no matter which house the child is in, and eliminate or at least greatly lessen arguments about their child, all of which will go far toward giving the child what they truly need—a loving, respectful, nourishing, safe, secure, and stable situation with each parent.

Platonic parents typically spend a lot of time planning for their potential child and creating such parenting plans. If you're planning to live apart from your child's other parent, it would be wise to do the same.

Philadelphia resident Charles Bourne lives with his husband about twenty minutes away from his platonic coparent, with whom he has twin daughters. The girls share equal time with both parents. But they aren't figuring out things on their own—they have turned to a family therapist to help them navigate issues of raising their twins while living separately.[238]

"That level of thoughtfulness really benefits kids—these are people who have thought about how do I want to raise a child, whom do I want to raise a child with—that can only be good for children," notes Jennifer Chrisler, former executive director of Family Equality Council, a national advocacy organization for the LGBTQ+ community. "We should all think that hard about how we are going to have our kids and what we're going to do once they're in the world. If everybody gave that kind of thought to having children, we'd probably have better outcomes."[239]

In China, parents have been exploring various versions of live apart together relationships that consider children's needs first, but not without consequences. Some mothers willingly live apart from their husbands for the sake of their children during their educational years, becoming what's called "study mothers," described by one researcher as "women who physically accompany and take care of their children full-time to provide them with optimal living and study conditions, relocating their residences near their children's school."[240] While children get the full attention and support of their mother, some worry about their relationships with their father.

And in some wealthy provinces of China, an increasing number of couples have been choosing *liang tou hun*—two-sided marriage or separate marriage. Couples need to have two children for the marriage to work best, a possibility ever since China lifted the one-child-only policy in 2015. Not only do the couple live apart—the wife stays with her family, who help raise the child, while the husband stays with his family, who also help raise the child—but so do their children, although some couples switch between living with each set of parents.[241]

Clearly, there are many ways to live as a family. The key is tuning in to the needs of your child and trying to meet those needs continuously through their development, Carlsson-Paige says. "The way we arrange our living situation isn't as important as being able to relate to kids in developmentally appropriate ways through their lives."

9 | LET'S TALK ABOUT SEX

People across the globe are having less sex, or so one of the most comprehensive sex studies to date has discovered.[242]

Don't tell that to LAT couples.

"Living apart can boost sexual desire, which means that, even though you're not living together, you experience greater sexual frequency and satisfaction as a couple," says Australian sex and relationship therapist Isiah McKimmie.[243]

"Even the sex becomes that much more intense. Because we want to make the best use of those two days, we live our lives more fully," Bidisha Das, in a LAT relationship for three years, tells *Vice*.[244]

"I accept as human nature that we're always going to have desires. But if you get a desire satisfied, another one takes its place. I'd rather be in a state of desire for her than have her there all the time. Maybe I like that bit of frustration of not seeing her as much as I think I'd want," says David Scribner, who has lived in another state from his romantic partner for more than two decades.[245]

But are Das's and Scribner's experiences universal for all live apart together couples? Couldn't going days, weeks, or perhaps even months not seeing each other create trouble—frustration, temptation, jealousy, insecurity?

"When [couples] are long-distance, it can lead to frustrations and sexual buildup that shows in other parts of their relationship," says sex therapist Nazanin Moali, host of the *Sexology* podcast.[246]

Jealousy and insecurity can be big obstacles for some couples, says therapist and longtime LAT partner Judye Hess. "Before you take this step, you have to be really secure in your relationship. The commitment you need in your relationship can't be half-assed. It takes more trust when you're not going to see the person and you have no idea what they're doing all day or night."[160]

E. A. Marconi, who lived apart from her husband of thirty years in separate units in his duplex, agrees.

"I don't see how this type of LAT will work if one person still deals with jealousy in part because they aren't experienced," she says. "There's a certain confidence one has if you've been around the block to know if you're ready to settle down. I believe it takes a strong, mature person to LAT and not have trust issues."[163]

Trust is essential, psychologist and relationship expert Sherrie Sims Allen tells me. You build trust by keeping your word, which is what she counted on when she and her husband lived apart for many years. "And the beauty is we're now in a digital age. People can be on Zoom, on FaceTime. You have many ways in which to stay connected and be connected as a couple. Keeping integrity, keeping one's word, honoring the relationship. My husband and I always say, put the relationship first. Making sure the health of the relationship is in place."[119]

As we saw in Chapter 3, just because you live apart from your romantic partner doesn't mean that you're more likely to cheat on them or vice versa. Again, if you can't trust your partner and they can't trust you, your living arrangement isn't going to change anything.

According to Dr. Gregory Guldner, author of *Long Distance Relationships: The Complete Guide,* "the risk of having an affair is related more to the quality of the relationship between the couple, and the personalities involved, than on mere opportunity."[247]

Still, certified sex coach Gigi Engle observes that it takes effort. "If you're not working to keep your sexuality connected to your partner when you can't physically touch them, it becomes less of a romantic relationship. You lose the intimacy that you have when you're with someone in real life."[248]

GETTING CREATIVE

Living apart from your romantic partner *is* real life in my mind. Clearly, though, the way to make sure you and your partner are getting everything you want sexually from your LAT relationship is to do whatever you can to boost communication and intimacy, together or apart.

"There's a sacrifice of day-to-day intimacy, both emotional and sexual," says couples therapist Ili Rivera Walter, owner of CityCouples, an online therapy practice.[162]

Which is why LAT couples may need to get creative to maintain their intimate and sexual relationship when they're not together.

"Being innovative, whatever that means to the couple, sexting or using technology to have sexual encounters with one another," she says. "Communication around this area is crucial—what can flirting look like, what can sexting look like, what is good timing, can they actually schedule long-distance sexual encounters if that's going to be part of their repertoire when they're apart?"

This is especially important if you live in different time zones. You may not want to get a sext or naked photo from your LAT partner when you're at the office, meeting with a client, or putting your young child to bed.

Of course, there are many new sex toys that enable couples to be sexually connected from afar, such as remote-controlled vibrators and app-controlled toys. There's even something called the Kissing Device, an app with silicone lips that can supposedly replicate the pressure, movement, and temperature of your lips—even the smooching sound—so you can kiss your LAT partner when you're apart.[249]

Granted, some may find such technology creepy, but others embrace it. Finding your comfort level is important.

Eric Marlowe Garrison, a certified sexuality counselor, likes to talk about the importance of maintaining what he calls "simmer" when you live apart from your partner. "How do we keep things at a simmer so when we need to turn them up to a boil, it's a lot easier than starting from a pan of ice-cold water," he tells me.[250]

Simmer can include all the usual suspects mentioned above—texting, sexting, apps, etc.—as well as other creative connections. A few couples Garrison has worked with kept a continuous piece of erotica going, with one writing some of the story and the other adding onto it before passing it back—"almost like a sexual pen pal piece." And because it's all about fantasy, "any things that they feel need to be remedied can be remedied through fantasy." Can't see each other for a while? You can in your fantasy.

INTIMACY BOOST

Despite the mistaken belief held by many that LATs aren't faithful or monogamous, sexual fidelity is often considered the most important expression of commitment for them. In fact, as researcher Alexandra-Andreea Ciritel observes, "in the absence of joint investments, such as buying a house, paying the mortgage together, and having children, sex may be a more important investment and valued resource for LATs, and this may explain why they enjoy greater sexual intimacy than coresidential couples."[251]

Yes, you read that right—"greater sexual intimacy than coresidential couples."

Of course, some LAT couples do have joint investments, such as children or houses or other property. And some researchers have found that sex may not even be all that important for how LATs define their relationship. A study by University College London professor Sasha Roseneil suggests that, for some LATs, having a sexual partner who may not last lifelong may not be as important as investing "time and energy in maintaining friendships" to have a happy, more secure life.[252] (More on that in Chapter 12.)

Ciritel also finds that, as counterintuitive as it may seem, "High levels of sexual satisfaction are important in decisions to remain living apart (and perhaps to sexually experience and test the relationship)."[253]

And people who enjoy being sexually intimate with their LAT partner experience that as part of the "rewards" they get from their relationship and thus are much more willing to make sure their relationship lasts.[72]

Passion plays a part, as sociologists Bernadette Bawin-Legros and Anne Gauthier discovered. "Often invoked in nonresidential couples, passion becomes freedom of action requiring no justification, neither of itself, nor of its consequences."[143]

One couple who never lived under the same roof during their twenty-five-year marriage and who also raised two children together were New York City author Judith Newman and her late husband, John Snowdon. Fourteen years into their marriage, when their twin sons were six years old, Newman addressed the misperceptions that a married couple who do not live together "must not be happy or ever have sex" or that they're having lots of sex, just not with each other.

"The notion that two people can live apart and still be in a traditional marriage, neither celibate nor throwing key parties, seems to make folks' head explode. To which I can only reply, in my own head, 'That's logical. We have separate places, so we must never have sex. Because as everyone knows, the thing that makes for a hot sex life is proximity,'" she writes.[234]

And she brings up something many LAT couples discover— they aren't constantly faced with the things about each other that they don't particularly like, which certainly fuels the mystery that's often the secret sauce of long-term relationships.

"If you live apart from someone and trust him, you have intimacy without that incestuous feeling that comes from too much information, which can lead couples to stop having sex."

Science actually backs her up. According to a 2017 study, "Partners who live apart are less likely to discover undesirable characteristics about one another."[254]

Is this something wrong with that? No. As one fiftysomething man in a LAT relationship shares, "We are told that 'it's selfish,' the way we live, because we only see the best in each other. It's true, greater attention is given to the other in the way we structure our couple because we don't have to see each other, it's not imposed by an external force. . . . We invite each other over and that forces us to make an effort."[143]

The same 2017 study says that there's lots of research that demonstrates that maintaining a romantic relationship isn't necessarily all about being together but how you reflect on it. "The way partners think about their relationships/partners has as much or more to do with relationship maintenance as do their interactions."

And if that isn't enough to convince you, researchers from the

University at Buffalo and the University of British Columbia found that people who have a positive view of their romantic partner (whether they deserve it or not)—what the study calls "unrealistic idealization"—were happier and more satisfied in their relationship than those who saw them as they actually were.[255]

They weren't talking about LAT couples per se, but it seems to apply to their experience. As we saw in Chapter 1, social psychologist Samantha Joel discovered that LAT couples often experience more passion, idealize their partners more, daydream about their relationship, and report more loving feelings toward their partner than couples who live together.[49]

For writer Annie Fox, living apart from her husband allows her to explore her sexuality solo.

"Having the luxury of time and space (I like to treat the whole bed like a picnic rug and lay out all the things I might need) makes masturbating a real pleasure. Plus, it gives me the opportunity to try out new things free from the anxiety that someone might come home early and walk in on me in an Elsa costume."[256]

All that juicy solo time can only benefit their relationship, even if he never gets to see her dressed up as a character from Disney's 2013 movie *Frozen*.

INTENTIONS, NOT EXPECTATIONS

That said, it isn't always a (separate) bed of sexual roses for LAT couples, or so Garrison tells me.[250]

"I like to say that relationships like this need some latitude," says Garrison, who's worked with many LAT couples from his New York City office. "So often sex is so much easier to do than talk about. You're not going to have a great relationship in the bedroom if you can't talk about it in the dining room."

There may be pressure to be sexual when you finally see each other, even if, sometimes, one of you is not in the mood, he says.

Or too tired, stressed, worried, jet-lagged, upset, sad, sick, or any of the other reasons people sometimes aren't on the same sexual page.

That could be especially disappointing for LAT couples who live far from each other and have to travel long distances to be together and, boom—they're confronted with an unexpected illness or other libido killer.

"I really encourage people to throw away expectations and replace them with intentions," he says. "And also look at what is optimal versus what is maximal."

What does that mean?

If intercourse isn't in the cards when you're together, ask yourself what you can create to optimize pleasure and intimacy for both of you.

Rather than go for a cookie-cutter intimate experience—"sex must look like this"—recognize that "today sex is going to look like a little bit A, a little bit of C, and a little bit of F, whereas last week it was a lot of K and whole lot of X, Y, and Z."

It can happen to LAT couples who live close by, too. As Hess explained in Chapter 5, when her romantic partner moved near her shortly after they met, he began sleeping over her place every night, creating a sexual rut that was unhappy for her. Hess eventually set some healthy boundaries.[160]

And, as we saw in Chapter 4, the judgment of others can get in the way of how LAT couples express themselves sexually.

Still, there is no way to gauge intimacy without the backdrop of what's considered normal, acknowledge Bawin-Legros and Gauthier. "The life of a nonresidential couple depends, then, on the way in which it manages its intimacy and external norms, rendered concrete through the eyes of others."

Like child development expert Nancy Carlsson-Paige, Garrison is a big fan of rituals to reconnect to your partner after some time apart, even small things like taking a bath or shower or walking together. And, he says, having a ritual *before* the ritual.

Meaning you talk about the somewhat mundane day-to-day goings-on ahead of time so when you're together you're not having to ask questions, he says. "Those things are out of the way. Not to say that they're superficial but that time you're together, the quality is there.

"At some point, while you're physically together or before you're physically together, take an hour and you communicate to each other with, 'I need less of, I need more of, and I really liked it when.' It's done in 'I' statements, and it can be just about sex—'I need less tongue in ear and more tongue in my mouth, and I really loved it when we French-kissed for like an hour after we saw that movie the other night.' And you let each other run through their entire list before you ask for clarification. You don't interrupt, you listen, you receive."

He also suggests LAT couples know that they can do things separately even when they're together.

"It's a mindset of, 'It's OK for us to do things apart while we're together.' A lot of people think because you're LAT that you have to spend every waking minute together when you're together," he says.

And that includes sex.

Couples can agree that "we don't have to have a whole weekend of sex just because we're together this weekend."

Of course, they can just as easily decide that they want to.

10 | UNTIL DEATH DO YOU PART . . . APART?

If you're going to live happily apart forever, that means you'll be aging apart. Or will you?

Would you prefer to move in together at a certain age, or if one or both of you become ill or disabled, or if an illness or disability progresses, or do you intend to keep things as is? What if one of you wants to move in together but the other doesn't? What will your decision mean for caregiving? How much caregiving do you want to give or expect to get? In what way might your or your partner's children impact your arrangement? How will you manage retirement?

There's no right or wrong way to approach living apart together arrangements in the later years of life and the amount of caregiving you intend to provide or not, however, there's a societal expectation that spouses and adult children will be the primary caregivers as a person ages. Although there's scant research about what LAT partners decide, the few studies available indicate many LATs are flexible when it comes to looking after their romantic partner later in life.

About half of the couples responding to a small 2015 Dutch study said they planned to offer care for their romantic partner if needed, which could be interpreted as a good number of LAT people having ambivalence about caregiving. Still, when their partners actually became ill, they helped, nonetheless. So perhaps while living apart independently is a couple's preference, they could see moving in together to give care as a necessity.[257]

A more recent study led by Jacquelyn Benson, an assistant professor of human development and family science at the University of Missouri, found that many single but committed couples aged sixty and older are "willing to make changes in living arrangements to provide caregiving support to one another," and even live together, especially if their relationship would end if they didn't.[254] But she cautions that until the day someone is confronted with their own or a partner's major illness or disability, it's impossible to know what, if any, changes they will actually make.

"Most of the individuals we interviewed had not been tested by the realities of caregiving within their current LAT partnerships. It will be important to follow LAT partners over time to see if their willingness transforms into action and understand the mechanisms that explain these care provision decisions," Benson notes.[258]

It isn't just about caregiving. If you're planning to transition from living apart to living together, it isn't always seamless. Not only do you have to discard or meld personal items from separate housing with sensitivity to each other's needs, but you also need to create a space where both of you feel at home. Other things that need to be considered are financial responsibilities, division of housework, hosting friends and family, communication about comings and goings, solo time, and other lifestyle preferences that living without a partner allows you to enjoy.

Obviously, how much caregiving you're willing to offer—or not—for your romantic partner as they age, and how much you expect from them, will be up to you. But one thing is certain: you'll need to talk about aging and retirement and how that might impact your LAT relationship, as well as something few of us like to talk about—end-of-life planning.

E. A. Marconi was the sole caregiver for her husband of thirty years, Mason, at the end of his life. They had no children, and their families lived far away. "While it is something I would never wish on anyone, it felt good to be able to give him that," she tells me.[163]

Diagnosed with pancreatic cancer that radiation didn't help, Mason chose to bring in hospice while waiting for approval for a legal prescription for life-ending medication.

Although she describes their LAT arrangement as perfect when he was healthy—they had separate units in his duplex, connected by a spiral staircase—it became a bit challenging once he became ill.

"I was constantly going up and down stairs to take care of him and deal with my own stuff," she tells me. Fortunately, she had no health or mobility issues that would make that challenging. It might be daunting if she did. That is something to consider.

Distance and ease of visitation as you age may be something you and your LAT partner may want to discuss and plan for.

Therapist Judye Hess is a lot older than her longtime romantic partner. Both being baby boomers and childfree, they haven't talked about future caregiving needs—it's an unspoken contract, she tells me—but she believes they'll show up for each other.[160] While they have advance directives and she is clear that she'd like to leave money to her favorite nonprofits and some to her partner, she doesn't have a will. She knows she should have one.

"I just hate working with paperwork and making those decisions. So, I'm just procrastinating," she says. "I'm just 'when push comes to shove, I'll take care of it.' But it's something I really need to do."

In her late sixties and with a husband in his late seventies, *Living Happily Ever After—Separately* author Lise Stoessel is anticipating the future. Sometime in the next ten or fifteen years, she tells me, she can see herself moving back into his house; his house is one floor and better for aging in place than hers. There are practicalities to consider, she says.[149]

"I can imagine this scenario is going to shift if one or the other of us needs more hands-on support," she says. "If either of us becomes debilitated or incapacitated, the hope and expectation is that the other one would be there to offer support."

That said, she's clear about maintaining her independence, the reason why they became LATs in the first place some fifteen years ago. "If it's a matter of my having to caregive him, I would absolutely need to make provisions for breaks, or maybe nights at my own place or whatever," she says.

Author Judith Newman never lived with her late husband, who was thirty years older, throughout their twenty-five years of marriage, until he was diagnosed with three types of cancer—pancreatic, liver, and prostate. That's when she moved him into a hospital bed she set up in her bedroom in her New York City apartment, where she cared for him until he died shortly after.

"I had decided to go full pioneer woman and tend to him myself. I'm still not sure why. Normally I am the queen of outsourcing. Also, I am a terrible nurse. But my decision to care for him at home was made in an instant. He wanted to be here. Our 16-year-old twins . . . desperately wanted him here. And so did I," she writes in her 2018 *Modern Love* column.[259]

Neither Hess nor Stoessel has plans set in stone, which might worry people like Benson.

"Discussions about end-of-life planning and caregiving can be sensitive to talk about; however, LAT couples should make it a priority to have these conversations both as a couple and with their families. Many of us wait until a crisis to address those issues, but in situations like LAT, where there are no socially prescribed norms dictating behavior, these conversations may be more important than ever."[260]

WHEN CHILDREN ARE THE PROBLEM

An important reason to have those discussions comes from a perhaps unexpected source—your adult children. Having minor children at home factors into parents' repartnering decisions. Surprisingly, it doesn't always change as the children reach adulthood. But whereas a young child might not have much control over whom their parent repartners with and how, adult children have much more power and often aren't afraid to exert it.

When Northern California author Eve Pell married a widower when she was seventy-one and he was eighty-one, she initially found resistance from his children—"That was a huge surprise," she tells me. Many of the couples who shared their stories with her for her book, *Love, Again: The Wisdom of Unexpected Romance*, had similar responses.[261]

Some adult children were content with their family "as is," with a single parent or parents. Some feared a new romantic partner would take time or inheritance or both away from them and their children. Some adult children didn't want to let go of memories of their childhood and their parents' marriage and how things had always been.

Adult stepchildren can be as resentful as younger children, notes Wednesday Martin, author of *Stepmonster: A New Look at Why Real Stepmothers Think, Feel, and Act the Way We Do.* "As the kids get older, issues like estate planning and inheritance can come into play, adding an extra layer of anxiety and resentment," she writes.[262]

While experts advise that you need to take your adult children's feelings into account and be sensitive to their concerns— without giving them the upper hand—some adult children may act poorly once a parent becomes ill or incapacitated.[263]

In a study of how adult children and stepchildren impact their divorced or widowed parents' romantic decisions, researchers Jenny de Jong Gierveld and Eva-Maria Merz found that even LAT couples were impacted. They share a story of a sixty-seven-year-old man in a LAT relationship who was the sole caretaker for his terminally ill partner. Although her adult children did not help care for their ailing mother, they still denied his status as her romantic partner and primary caregiver and even excluded him from the preparations for her funeral.

"[H]er children did not even put my name on the memorial card," he told the researchers, heartbreakingly.[189]

In Benson's study, one woman only discovered that her LAT partner had been placed in a nursing facility by his family when she was unable to reach him at home. "They didn't include her in the conversation at all, and she was pretty upset about it," Benson says.[264]

Both those scenarios seem incredibly painful. It's important to consider your children's thoughts and feelings about a new LAT romantic partner. It's also essential to have conversations about caregiving and end-of-life planning early and often.

As Marconi shares, Mason didn't want anyone else to care for him besides her. But if they had children from their previous marriages, that decision may have been out of their hands, especially his desire to opt for physician-assisted death—a controversial issue for some.

Mason was not alone in wanting his female partner to look after him. There are cultural and social expectations that women do the caregiving, and research confirms that many women fulfill that role, sometimes at the risk of their own mental and physical health. Many women choose to live apart from a romantic partner specifically as a way to avoid the hands-on caregiving expected of them in a live-in arrangement.

"I think it's important for women to know it is OK to not want to serve as a caregiver and to still hold value as women in society," says Allison Forti, of Wake Forest University's counseling department.[265]

This may be particularly important to older Black women. In her doctoral dissertation, Nytasia Hicks found that although some of the thirteen Black women she interviewed aged fifty-nine and older told her that they would provide physical support to their romantic partner, others were not interested in offering care if it in any way compromised their lifestyles and if it created an emotional, financial, or physical burden. They prioritized their role as their family's provider, caretaker, or parent over their role as a LAT partner.[266]

Although informal caregiving is seen as the responsibility of the family in African cultures versus relying on paid care services, they did not plan to provide long-term caregiving without bringing in outside help. In fact, they barely talked with their LAT partners about caregiving expectations.

Forti suggests that if someone wants to avoid caregiving for their LAT partner, they should have a conversation at the beginning of a new relationship. One way to start the conversation, she says, is like this: "Having been a caregiver when my mother died, I want to discuss what we would do if one of us needed care." Be as detailed as you can and be open to what your partner—who may have different care expectations—has to say. And, experts suggest, share your wishes for your own care, whom you expect to do it, such as adult children or paid caregivers, and how you plan to pay for it.[265]

They also suggest drafting a caregiver agreement to spell out the specifics of care for each partner so everyone, including family members, is on the same page. You don't want to end up like the people in the studies detailed above, whose children worked behind a LAT partner's back to exclude them from long-term care and funeral planning.

EXPECTING THE UNEXPECTED

Caregiving and end-of-life planning aren't the only things to consider as you age as LATs. There's also retirement.

There are three things people have a hard time talking about, Dee Cascio, a certified retirement coach and licensed therapist, shares—money, sex, and retirement.[267]

As much as many people look forward to retirement, it can cause anxiety, not only from a loss of identity, fear of loneliness, and potential financial issues, but also from differing retirement timing and goals. Even if you are living apart from your romantic partner, you may find that how you want to spend your time in retirement may differ drastically from theirs.[268]

Take, for example, Patrick and Mary, a longtime LAT couple in Britain whom psychotherapist Pierre Cachia writes about in a chapter of the 2020 book *Couple Relationships in a Global Context*, edited by Angela Abela, Sue Vella, and Suzanne Piscopo. Both had been thinking about what retirement might look like. Patrick expressed a desire to live a more slow-paced life, without a lot of travel and stressful vacation planning. Mary, on the other hand, was imagining her retirement to be filled with activities and ticking off a long-desired travel bucket list.

"The very thought of joining him 'not doing very much' caused her to feel suffocated," Cachia notes.[269]

Planning for retirement is a challenge for almost all couples, but it's particularly challenging for LAT couples, Cachia tells me.[270] Having different goals for your retirement isn't necessarily the biggest issue they face, however; health and distance apart is.

If you live far from your LAT partner, transportation to see each other may become harder. It might be tempting to move in together, or at least move closer geographically to each other, but that might mean one or both of you will be far from family, friends, community, and perhaps long-established health care providers and medical offices. "That may be a major transition," he says. As we saw in Chapter 7, moving in together may not be a possibility if you're disabled and one or both of you are receiving disability benefits.

If one of you develops medical issues and the other partner envisioned a life of traveling in retirement, that could impact the freedom to do whatever you want, Cascio observes, "and not feel the guilt around not helping to take care of that partner or that relationship that you've had for a long time. There's a lot of emotional stuff that goes into this that people aren't prepared for."

But even if a LAT couple lives close enough to each other and is enjoying good health and mobility, how much time you want to spend together when you may have more time to do so can cause some anxiety, too. "For the first time, it's not about planning a weekend or two weeks together," Cachia says.

Aging, he acknowledges, can make LAT relationships become a bit less flexible. Which is why LATs should be prepared as best they can.

"It's much better if that preparation happens earlier than later," Cachia says. "It might be anything from shifting medical support centers, preparing family and friends for the transition, talking about the loss that will come from any shift in the shared LAT lifestyle. If a couple lives some distance away, they have to manage the distance. But if they no longer live some distance away, then they have to manage the proximity, and proximity can be as much of a headache."[270]

Finances are another thing to consider if you and your partner have substantial differences in retirement savings, says Cascio, or if one of you is retired and the other has to keep working because they need the income. "They may be limited in how much they can do with their retired partner," she says. They may need to split those kinds of expenses proportionally versus fifty-fifty, as discussed in Chapter 6.

LATS FORCED APART

Another thing to plan for is the possibility of one or both of you moving into a continuing care retirement community (CCRC) or starting a new LAT relationship while already living in such a community.

In her research on widows who met a new romantic partner after moving into a CCRC, University of Haifa gerontologist Chaya Koren discovered that LAT couples tend to downplay their relationship, calling it a "friendship" over a "partnership," as a way to minimize judgment, envy, and jealousy, and as a way to balance a sense of belonging to the larger group. Although some can move into a unit together, many resist. Residents and perhaps even some staff members in such care communities do not always approve of late-life repartnering, her research indicates, in part because it doesn't seem age-appropriate and in part because it appears disrespectful to the deceased spouse.[271]

And, because women typically live longer than men, the majority of people living in a CCRC are white, widowed elderly women, making it harder for a heterosexual female resident to find a male romantic partner.[272]

As Koren notes, "LAT partners in the community outside the

CCRC do not have to give an account to an institutional social environment, and thus their lives remain more private than in the CCRC. As such, one of the disadvantages of a LAT relationship within an institutional environment is limited autonomy within the LAT relationship. As a result, being together all the time might become a burden rather than an asset because it restricts human freedom."[273]

It's even more challenging for LGBTQ+ people who'd like to be in a LAT relationship in a care community. They are often forced to hide their identity out of fear of bias, harassment, and being refused or getting reduced care if they can't find space in LGBTQ+-friendly senior housing.[274]

In fact, LGBTQ+ couples who live apart together may face challenges as they age even if they are still in their own homes. Many lesbian women and gay men choose to live apart from their romantic partners to maintain privacy about their relationship, which means family members may not know their partner—or know that they even have a romantic partner—or may question the legitimacy of their relationship.[68]

Canadian sociologist Ingrid Arnet Connidis raises important questions in her study of later-life LAT couples, whom she calls LLAT, as to how a LLAT partner is experienced by adult children and other relatives.[275]

"From the standpoint of adult children, the fact that a parent is LLAT cannot be assumed to mean future care for their parent if needed. What are the implications of this assumption for negotiating a relationship with a parent's LLAT partner? Is there an effort to develop an emotional bond in the absence of assuming an instrumental one? Does the expansion of networks that LAT potentially allows increase the number of potential care providers . . . or is there ambivalence among adult children about offering care to their parent's LLAT partner? Is a LLAT partner 'part of the family' or 'my parent's partner'? . . . In cases where LLAT partners do eventually provide care despite a starting assumption that this would not occur, are the family members, especially children, expected or likely to support their parents' caregiving efforts?"

Certainly, these are conversations to have with your children, your relatives, and your partner.

And there are unexpected realities that come if you've lived apart from your romantic partner after their death, Marconi tells me. Many widows and widowers in longtime live-in relationships may be living alone for the first time in decades—perhaps ever. Widows seem to fare better, research indicates.[275] Many relish a newfound sense of freedom, as Marti Benedetti and Mary A. Dempsey detail in their 2021 book *Finding Love After Loss: A Relationship Roadmap for Widows*.[276]

Marconi had freedom in her marriage, she shares. So it was surprising for her to realize that when someone has a relationship that offers love and commitment as well as space to breathe, it's a different kind of grieving, one that others may not understand.

"I tend to feel depressed when I read about all of these women who find themselves alone later in life and find a new sense of freedom. I'm thinking, 'Why am I not feeling this?' It's because I had my freedom all along. Seriously, he and I were totally supportive of one another's drive to be our own person and do our own things," she tells me.

"I think the traditional widow would feel more lonely if their relationship was more dependent on the other, but I can't imagine anyone feeling more alone in the world than I do at times."[277]

11 | CAN THIS MARRIAGE BE SAVED?

Telegraph journalist Celia Walden created a bit of a kerfuffle when she wrote about taking a six-week sabbatical from her marriage to British broadcaster Piers Morgan. As with many couples, the pandemic proved to be too much time together for her. "[W]hen you consider how unnatural it was to spend every waking hour in your other half's company for all those long months, it's a miracle any couple—married or not—made it through unscathed," she wrote. "[E]very married couple (who has lived through three lockdowns) should do this."[278]

Joan Anderson famously wrote about her yearlong sabbatical when she turned fifty in her best-selling 1999 book, *A Year by the Sea: Thoughts of an Unfinished Woman*, which became a movie in 2016, and the aftermath of that decision in 2002's *An Unfinished Marriage*. Anderson has been leading women's retreats ever since and believes that if a couple was truly in love and felt excited to be together early in their relationship, "then couples can find it with each other again."[279]

The term *marriage sabbatical* wasn't first mentioned until 2000, when journalist Cheryl Jarvis wrote *The Marriage Sabbatical: The Journey that Brings You Home*, in which she describes the three months she spent away from her husband the year she turned forty-eight and details the experiences of fifty-five women, as well as historical figures such as Harriet Beecher Stowe, who also temporarily escaped their marriages to nurture themselves.

More recently, author Ruby Warrington credits her eight-month sabbatical with saving her marriage, calling it a "window of self-discovery and a crucial chapter" in their relationship, she wrote in 2017. And it felt like she and her husband were doing something brave: "The empty space we'd created had allowed us to see each other as individuals again. I was also reminded why I chose to be with my husband in the first place."[280]

So, if three or eight months or a year apart can salvage a marriage, can the same be said of deciding to live separately permanently?

That's what writer Leigh Shulman believes. She and her husband had been together for thirty years and had two children together when the pandemic changed everything, she writes in *Insider*. Like Walden, the togetherness was too much for her.[281]

The two spend most of the week apart and split caring for their children as if they were separated. It felt wrong at first, like spending time apart meant the end of them as a couple. But it gave her space to breathe, she says. She doesn't want to go back to living together.

One of the biggest challenges of their arrangement is dealing with what others think—the look of pity in others' eyes, she writes. The assumption is that their living apart from each other is because someone's being selfish or something is wrong with their marriage, but she says it makes their connection stronger.

Not to say that living apart should be the first thing a struggling couple does.

"Habituation really is when your partner becomes the couch. You walk in and you don't even notice the couch anymore—it's just there. If that is something that's happened to you, sure—this creates novelty. 'This is something new we're trying.' Again, that's a big leap," says therapist Heather "Lulu" Mazzei.[122]

"If you're trying to save the marriage, that might not be my first suggestion. If you haven't done couples' therapy, if you haven't done individual therapy, if you haven't tried to create more novelty in the relationship, I would start with those things. But if you've done all that and you're thinking, yeah, we still have this companionship, love, and we want to keep it, it could be an interesting option to explore. But again, this has to happen with so much gentleness. Is it both people's idea? And if it's not both people's idea, if only one person wants it, then how's that going to work?"

It did work for Lise Stoessel, whom we met in Chapter 4, whose husband, Emil, was not pleased with the idea when she first presented it to him, as she details in her book *Living Happily Ever After—Separately.*

But it was either that or a divorce, she says. Except she didn't really want to leave him—she just needed some space.[282] And Emil began to realize that divorce would be a lot more expensive than living apart.[283]

So, she got her own house. Now they see each other about six days a week and spend about four nights a week together. They've been doing it for the past fifteen years of their more than thirty-year marriage.

"It's given us the breathing space. Instead of being constantly irritated by the things we don't like about the other person, we miss and appreciate the things we love. We no longer have a battle of conflicting needs because we each have our own space," she says.

It did save her marriage, she says. Which is why she suggests others may want to consider it.

"I would recommend it to anyone who is having issues with compatibility in their marriage. Not everyone needs to live separately," she shares. "I wish we could live happily together, but we can't. Fortunately, we found out that we can still be very married, still support and nurture each other, and keep our family intact, by living separately."[282]

It also worked for Missouri couple Jeff and Connie Ordway, who had been married for eighteen years when Connie suggested she get her own place. After the pandemic stay-at-home orders, which stressed many couples, Connie realized their rural home, which benefited their children, was too isolating for her. So, in March 2022, she got an apartment about twenty minutes away from her husband, and they see each other a few times a week.

"I am a mother. I am a wife. I am a farmer. I don't know where I fit. Where's the me part?" she told *The New York Times*.[284]

Now, she not only is rediscovering the me part, but it has also revived their marriage. "It feels like we're dating again," she observes.

Freelance writer Crystal Hammon writes that after twenty-five years of marriage, she and her husband were basically two people sharing the same roof. "We loved each other deeply and we shared common goals and interests, but we didn't exactly *like* each other." That may sound familiar to anyone in a long-term marriage or relationship.[285]

When she rented and eventually bought a one-bedroom condo about ninety minutes from their family home—dubbed

"The Treehouse"—their relationship got better and more spontaneous. Hammon realized how much she enjoyed living alone, and she observed that her husband was "more attentive" and "less grumpy." Their interactions were more intentional.

Sometimes, living apart together to salvage a marriage ends with a couple moving back in together. Still, the experience prompts couples to find ways to make space in their relationship to encourage and support agency and autonomy.

That was true for Sana and Adnan Akhand.

In January 2022, Sana Akhand posted a video on TikTok that went viral about how she and her husband had decided to live apart to salvage their seven-year marriage, which had fallen into a rut and typical gendered patterns. Although they had agreed to live apart for up to three years, they moved back in together after just eight months, after they relocated to Los Angeles from New York City for Adnan's new job.[286]

It wasn't an easy adjustment at first, she shares. But they worked through it by making sure each of them had time for themselves, doing their own things Mondays through Thursdays and then spending time together on the weekends.

Sana says she'd consider living apart again, but not if they have children. But she's incredibly proud of their bold decision.

"We both have so much independence to enjoy our own hobbies, boundaries for alone time, respect for each other to pursue our individual dreams and so much more love connection and intimacy together because we finally get to see the most authentic and powerful version of each other. And damn it's so sexy," she wrote on her Instagram. "I'm so damn glad we took the risk and came back together stronger than ever."[287]

It was a similar experience for Rebecca Huff, who writes at *That Organic Mom*, and her husband, Shawne. She suggested to her husband of nearly two decades that they live apart—what she calls a healing separation—because their marriage was suffering after ignoring problems for years despite going to therapy and trying to make things work.[288]

First they lived in separate parts of their house. Then they lived apart for two years—she and their daughter in an apartment above his unit, which he shared with their son. Both enjoyed the freedom it offered.

Until the pandemic hit. They moved back in together in early 2021.[289]

Still, their time apart revived their marriage. As Huff shares on the *Home. Made.* podcast, "We had repaired our relationship to the point where we felt we could not just tolerate living together, but that we could actually enjoy it."[290]

Like with the Akhands, it wasn't an easy adjustment at first. But Huff, too, relied on boundaries to ensure that she was getting the time she needed to have for herself. "It's not selfish of me to ask for a couple of hours to have time to myself."

And, like Sana, she would consider it again. "I don't think that a married couple has to live together to have a good relationship. I fully believe that two people can be completely in love with one another, have every intention of staying together for the rest of their lives, and still enjoy living in separate spaces," she shares.

What's clear from their stories is that, like in most situations, both partners must be on the same page to want to experiment with their living arrangement.

Even if both people are on the same page, living apart to save a marriage doesn't always work, however. British journalist and author Tim Lott and his former wife were heading toward a divorce in 2013 when the idea of living apart together came up. They tried it for almost two years. It was wonderful at first. They fought less, and it even started to feel a bit romantic. But it didn't feel like the answer, he writes in *The Guardian*. "Rather than a bold experiment in a new way of living, it felt neither here nor there. There was always a question at the back of my mind—how is this going to end?"[291]

Believing there was enough "there" there, he moved back into the family home. They lasted another year before finally divorcing. He doesn't see their experiment as a failure, however.

"I think anyone whose relationship is struggling—certainly when children are involved—needs to give everything they can to engineering a possible solution. This may include counselling, therapy, meditation, or living apart together—whatever it takes. We tried them all—and they were all worth trying."

TALKING IT THROUGH

One thing people who try living together before deciding to live apart say is that they had lots of honest but hard conversations about how cohabiting wasn't working for them and that it wasn't really what they wanted, even if they thought they did. As you might expect, those conversations brought them emotionally if not physically closer. Many say that is how they continue to stay together—by staying apart.

As we saw in Chapter 3, having two separate spaces isn't necessarily more expensive than living together. But even if it were, Hammon considers the purchase of her condo an investment in her marriage and not an expense.

Divorce is expensive, she notes, but living apart is a lot less expensive and destructive. And it seems important to note that very few couples stay in the same housing situation once they divorce, which means one or both of you will have to find a place of your own. Why wouldn't living apart be a consideration if it was a way to keep your romantic partnership intact? It also begs the question—what are you willing to do to make your marriage better suit you and your needs right now?

As psychologist and relationship expert Sherrie Sims Allen tells me, "If the LAT model is an alternative to divorce, I think it saves money."[119]

A trial separation can strengthen a marriage, says Susan Pease Gadoua, a therapist and author of *Contemplating Divorce: A Step-by-Step Guide to Deciding Whether to Stay or Go*, as long as it's being done in the right way, for the right reasons, and with clear agreements and goals.[292]

Gadoua lays out what she considers the right way, which she calls an "Enhancement Separation": seek help from a neutral third party, especially if there are tensions or complications in the relationship; set boundaries and reasonable expectations; be sure you both have the same goal for separating, which is to better your marriage; and stay connected with your partner and agree on the ways to communicate.

As Gadoua says, many couples enjoy living apart from each other for a few months so much that they make it permanent. And save their marriage along the way.

Therapist Judye Hess, who has lived apart from her partner for more than twenty-four years, sometimes brings up the possibility of couples becoming LATs when counseling her clients, but not for everyone.[160]

"I don't recommend it out of the blue. It really has to come from them," she says. "I would really want to explore the fears on both sides. There's a lot to negotiate. It has to do with, I think, how much time together and how much time apart," she says.

Sims Allen and her husband, Melvin, did the opposite—they went from living on opposite coasts for five years to moving in together. But the experience of living apart continues to positively impact their relationship and their counseling practice. "The need for self-care and the need to pull away and to get perspective," she says. "We still keep that need to take a separate vacation or that time away. . . . We value each other's time alone to reflect and to exercise self-care and to 'do you.'"[119]

Still, they have suggested to some couples that they try living apart together to make their partnership work. But, she shares, it will only work if there's still a deep enough connection.

"I would hope they're in therapy while they're in a LAT relationship. I would hope that they're scheduling some we time, time to talk about how they've changed. Couples who married young, twenty years in and you're different people. Talk about that," she says. "Find ways to reconnect and get that sweet love back. You can't get innocent love back, but you can get mature love, where there's an appreciation. The friendship is the core piece of any relationship, a genuine friendship—'I like being around you.'

"This is an alternative. We're always looking for alternative solutions to having relationships work."

YOUR BEDROOM, MY BEDROOM

Another way couples are saving their romantic relationships is by sleeping separately, often called (distressingly) a "sleep divorce." As TV personality Carson Daly explained in 2020, sleeping in separate bedrooms from his wife, Siri—which they started doing when she was pregnant with their fourth child—is "the best thing that ever happened to us. We both, admittedly, slept better apart.... I don't know if we'll ever sleep together again."[293]

Did it save their marriage (and I am not saying that their marriage needed saving)? Who knows? That said, mismatched sleep patterns and needs can stress a romantic relationship. It did for Jennifer Adams. As she details in her 2015 book, *Sleeping Apart Not Falling Apart*, she was forced to break up with a former boyfriend who was a prolific snorer and liked to keep the bedroom frigid. Her sleep and health were suffering, even after she got a prescription for sleeping pills—a situation she wasn't too happy about. Her boyfriend suggested that she sleep with earplugs and dismissively advised her to "get over it."[294] Their sleep issues in part led to the demise of their relationship.

When she met the man who became her husband, that sleep situation almost replicated itself—until they decided to sleep in separate rooms. It's not for everyone, she acknowledges, but they both agreed that "being resentful towards the other person because one of us had to give up the when and how of sleeping wouldn't have made for a healthy relationship."

According to research, people who sleep fewer than seven hours a night tend to argue in a hostile, negative way. But if even just one person has a restful night's sleep, they and their partner were better able to find a peaceful, constructive resolution.[295]

"Prioritize sleep as a couple. Think of it as an investment in your relationship, because you really are a better partner as well as more productive and healthier and happier when you sleep better," says Wendy M. Troxel, a senior behavioral and social scientist at the RAND Corporation who coined the term *sleep alliance* as a kinder, gentler, and more realistic description of couples who sleep apart than *sleep divorce*. "If you have challenges with sleeping together, talk about it in a healthy and calm and honest way, instead of what I often see is out of desperation, one member of the couple abandons the bed, leaving the other partner to feel literally abandoned."[296]

In her 2020 TEDx talk, "How to Sleep Like Your Relationship Depends on It," Troxel says, "All of us need to make healthy sleep a priority. Because healthy sleep can strengthen our relationships, whereas sleepless nights can bring relationship harm." Which could perhaps lead to divorce if you're married or a relationship breakup, à la Adams.[297]

Couples who are mismatched in their sleep patterns and needs are more likely to have conflict and feel less satisfied in their romantic relationship. Can sleeping apart—whether in another room or another space—save your marriage/romantic relationship? Given what couples who have done it and experts who have researched it say, the answer seems to be yes.

That's not guaranteed. No one can predict how such things would impact your relationship unless you were working one-on-one with someone who has the tools to help you navigate a transition or you are self-aware and self-informed enough to be able to have those conversations on your own.

What Troxel states in her TEDx talk is that the key is to know how to negotiate your and your partner's differences and find a way to compromise.

All this assumes that things have not gotten so out of whack with your spouse/romantic partner that you are unable or unwilling to do that. When couples get to the "can this marriage be saved" phase of their relationship, there generally have been years, if not decades, of discontent.

It's about open and honest conversations—not a sleep divorce, but forging a sleep alliance with your partner.

Sleep, Troxel tells me, is among the many key aspects of a good relationship, even if it doesn't automatically come to mind. "Being poorly slept is definitely a risk factor for conflict in a relationship, particularly the toxic kinds of conflict," such as being hostile or withdrawn.[166]

A sleep alliance is saying, "We both recognize our need for sleep, and if doing it together doesn't serve that need, then we're open to other flexible solutions," Troxel says. "That doesn't necessarily mean something negative about the relationship; rather, it's a relationship-promoting activity—'We care so much about this relationship that we're willing to problem-solve.'"

Couples who decide to sleep apart to better their relationship remind me of the couples I interviewed for *The New I Do* who experimented with ethical nonmonogamy: they felt like they were trying something new and bold, and they liked how that made them feel.

Sims Allen doesn't see sleeping separately—no matter what you call it—as coming close to being a LAT couple. "The LAT relationship has a lot to do with space, your personal space, and certain couples don't want to share that space with their partner. They love their partner, they're committed, they just don't want to share."[119]

Not everyone has the chance to experience that, however. Some people never live on their own—they go from the family home to a dorm, to a shared apartment, to living with their romantic partner. In some countries such as Italy, Slovenia, Spain, and Greece, it's common for adult children to live with their parents until they wed.[298] The United States has seen a rise in young people, aged eighteen to twenty-nine, living with their parents, too, thanks in part to the 2008 recession and again during the coronavirus pandemic. If you don't get a chance to experience living on your own and you grow up believing romantic partners should sleep together, you may not know just how much space you need and what things you don't want to share with others.[299]

We saw two things impact relationships during the pandemic—that living 24–7 with a romantic partner stressed a lot of relationships, and that some couples who were forced to sleep/live apart temporarily, such as health care workers who were caring for COVID patients or a family member who came down with COVID and had to isolate themselves to protect their loved ones, came to realize that they actually liked the arrangement.

"It did open this window of opportunity, this aha moment for some couples who by circumstance needed to sleep apart during COVID," Troxel says. "This sort of forced occurrence allowed people to get over the stigma that they otherwise would not even consider or would be shamed."

So, an unplanned global event gave some couples a chance to experience a different way of being together. Couples can consciously choose that, too, especially if their sleep differences are stressing their partnership.

"Relationships that give you that solid foundation, that belief that your partner is and will be there for you in times of need, that actually becomes a cognitive schema. That's really the power of close relationships, that in theory, that attachment bond is there with you whether or not you're physically present with your partner," Troxel says.

When you have that foundation, that sense of safety and security, she says, it allows each of you to explore, grow, thrive—and even have a good night's sleep. Separately, of course.

12 | THE LAT REVOLUTION

If you did an Internet search of "live apart together" or "living apart together," you'd quickly get hundreds of thousands of results. Yet when you ask people about living apart from their romantic partner, many would ask, "Why?" Hopefully, after reading this book, you have a better understanding of why more are saying "why not?" to the LAT lifestyle and why they're embracing it, and if having a LAT relationship is right for you.

As I wrote in the introduction, and as this book has detailed, I am not saying having a LAT relationship is better than living together, nor am I advocating for couples to live apart. My goal is to let people know that they have options when it comes to creating a romantic relationship that best fits their needs, goals, and values.

Over the past fifty years, the number of people marrying in

the US has dropped by nearly sixty percent. In fact, marriage rates are falling across the globe.[300] More people are single, often by choice; single parents; cohabiting; having children outside of marriage; coparenting in platonic relationships; marrying multiple times; exploring polyamory and ethical nonmonogamy, and identifying as asexual and aromantic.[301] People across the world are disrupting the traditional linear approaches to forming intimate relationships—date, fall in love, move in together, marry. They are stepping off what author Amy Gahran calls the "relationship escalator."

"Only someone who is still filled with the [R]omanesque and romantic notion of love is surprised by the idea of two people who love one another lend no importance to shared activities or to a single shared living space. The way we feel about love today is perhaps more mature than that which sociological discourse tells us about it," write sociologists Bernadette Bawin-Legros and Anne Gauthier.[143]

The various ways of coupling are changing the romantic landscape and how we define family, highlighting how the social institutions that we've relied on for thousands of years can change relatively rapidly.[301]

However, as we have seen in this book, being single as population censuses define it doesn't necessarily mean there isn't a romantic partner—or partners—living nearby or far away. Until society knows more about LAT couples, we really won't be sure whether a desire for romantic or intimate partnerships is actually declining across the globe, as headlines often declare, or just transforming.[302] More importantly, if we aren't aware of these new ways of coupling, lawmakers and policymakers won't be able to identify how policies, rules, and regulations impacting such essential things as health care or housing can be more inclusive of LAT couples.

This matters because those who study the LAT lifestyle predict it will continue to attract more people, except in those parts of the globe where it's dangerous or almost impossible for young women to live solo, even if they have a romantic partner living elsewhere.

Many researchers hope that in the future, family surveys will include questions to identify LAT relationships, specifically asking questions to distinguish between those who are choosing the lifestyle versus those who become LAT couples due to constraints, and to tease out which LAT couples are in a committed romantic partnership versus those in more casual dating relationships. Research suggests that the rise in the number of people making a conscious choice to live apart from their romantic partner is "demographically and sociologically important and deserves attention."[118]

It does deserve attention, and actually more than that—it deserves policies that support the people who choose to live apart from their romantic partners. And it also deserves some good public relations so that more people can learn about it and consider it as a valid way to construct their romantic life without judgment and stigma, and so that the LAT lifestyle can be normalized.

CHANGING FAMILY FORMS

Many people, often conservatives, tend to wring their hands over the decline in marriage rates. What we are seeing, however, is that the narrow version of what society considers "family" often has outcomes many consider undesirable, including divorce, premarital cohabitation, children born to unwed couples, and multiple partnering. Sociologists observe that family forms are changing even in places such as China, Japan, Korea, and Taiwan—Asian societies that historically have emphasized the importance of strong family ties and family lineage—where there are also huge declines in marriage and fertility rates.[303]

Later or fewer marriages, and below-replacement fertility have huge implications for an aging population, they note, but the pronatalist policies those countries have embraced are not enough. Instead, they suggest, "policy efforts to promote family formation will have to move beyond efforts to promote work-family balance to change social institutions" to overcome long-held patriarchal and patrilineal beliefs within families, businesses, and government. Encouraging and supporting LAT relationships could just be an answer.

National University of Singapore sociologist Veronica L. Gregorio lays out some potential areas for sociologists to study when it comes to LAT relationships in the Philippines, where she's from, including how some couples prefer to live apart together as a way to avoid forming stepfamilies, as we saw in Chapter 8, and how some LGBTQ+ couples choose not to live together in a desire to keep their sexuality and romantic relationships private— important in a country like the Philippines, considered to be one of the most LGBTQ+-friendly countries in Asia despite being a deeply Catholic country. Gregorio also suggests that living apart together may be a good choice for unhappily married couples in the Philippines, where absolute divorce is illegal.[304]

As discussed in Chapter 7, some suggest opt-in legal protections for those in LAT relationships, including a way for LAT couples to register their partnerships if they want to formalize their romantic relationship.[199]

In a working paper suggesting policies to address changing family forms and relationships in contemporary Europe, the FamiliesAndSocieties project researchers call for legal and policy recognition of LAT relationships "with a focus on removing economic, social, and psychological constraints for such households to shape their own life courses."[305]

Because LAT is a growing lifestyle choice but one that is not taken into account by the United States Census and most other population surveys, prominent LAT researchers Simon Duncan, Miranda Phillips, Sasha Roseneil, Julia Carter, and Mariya Stoilova suggest that until that happens, those offering personal, health, and social care services, such as relationship and family counselors, need to better understand that being single doesn't automatically mean unpartnered, and that being partnered doesn't automatically mean the couple shares the same space.[202]

They also propose that technologies and services be designed to consider the needs of couples who are seeking to maintain intimate connections while living apart. Although not mentioned by the researchers, many streaming services have recently been threatening to nix sharing account passwords outside a household, which would negatively impact LAT couples wanting to have a Netflix-and-chill night together in their separate homes.[306]

Others advocate for designing housing and neighborhoods that would support alternative living arrangements.

"Right now, our homes and neighborhoods are designed for the nuclear family unit," says Rachel Hope, author of *Family by Choice: Platonic Partnered Parenting*, who has two children with two different coparents. "But going forward we may need new communal space, like compounds where platonic parents can coexist in close proximity to collectively raise children."[238]

Platonic parents wouldn't be the only ones to benefit from that kind of housing—LAT couples would, too, especially if they were co-raising minor children. Or multiunit housing. In 2018, Minneapolis was the first city to ban single-family home zoning, enabling duplexes and triplexes to be built in the same footprint of a single-family house.[307] Oregon became the first state to ban single-family home zoning in 2019,[308] followed by California in 2021.[309] Multiunit housing might be an attractive option for LAT couples who want to live close, but separate.

As sociologist Alisa C. Lewin observes, if more couples continue to become attracted to LAT relationships later in life, we need to better understand what living apart from one's partner means for their health, happiness, and well-being as a couple ages and the need for care and support increases. "They may need to devise other strategies for management of health and care. The policy implication is that older adults living apart from their partners need resources, guidance, and support to facilitate the self-management of their care."[73]

The number of people aged sixty-five or older is expected to increase exponentially by 2050, and the majority of them would prefer to age in place, according to research by McMaster University.[310] That could be accomplished with various housing models that support socializing and autonomy and offer access to essential services. That would go far in helping LAT couples as they age; older LAT couples who live far from each other may struggle with health or mobility issues or having easy access to affordable transportation, which could impact their union.

Although marriage and the nuclear family have long been idealized as the "right" household unit, sociologists Kathleen E. Hull, Ann Meier, and Timothy Ortyl question if a healthy, well-functioning society can exist without promoting marriage as the ideal. Their answer is unequivocally yes. There are other countries with fewer marriages and more cohabitation than the United States that are much more accepting of various models of intimacy, they write. "[S]ocial policy must be aligned with the types of relationships that individuals choose to form. Some of these countries extend significant legal protection and recognition to nonmarital relationships, and these countries do as well as, or sometimes better than, the US on key measures of social and familial well-being."[311]

That says a lot.

Although many couples thrive living under one roof, others don't, says Jacquelyn Benson, a researcher at the University of Missouri who has studied LAT couples. Society needs to accept that. "Do we expect that everyone would be good at parenting? That doesn't even make sense. Some people are not going to be great at it. It's the same thing as living together as a married couple—[some are] better at sharing space, compromising, and all those things," she says.[312]

As we've seen in this book, many heterosexual women, especially if they've lived with a male partner previously, often prefer to live on their own to avoid persistent gendered caregiving and housekeeping. But as more people are delaying marriage and even cohabitation, spending years living on their own has ramifications for their romantic relationships.

"When a couple come to live together, awareness of the pleasures of living alone can heighten efforts to attain fairness and awareness of the need to equalize belonging, ownership, and autonomy in command of space and time within their home and their relationship. If women experience living alone prior to living with a male partner, awareness of the balancing acts between self-identity and identity as a couple may help to enhance the gender equality of heterosexual relationships or at least heighten awareness of 'falling into gender,'" observes sociologist Lynn Jamieson.[313]

Instead of wringing our hands over the declining number of people interested in marrying and traditional ways of coupling, "We need to rethink how people can construct their relationships and maintain relationships not generally thought as normative," Benson says.[312]

ELDERS LEAD THE WAY

Interestingly, late-midlife and older LAT couples, what has been called later-life LAT (LLAT), are helping to drive the LAT revolution. "As a new form of intimate tie, LLAT challenges institutionalized intimate relationships and is more open to an uncluttered exploration of how intimate relationships are negotiated," one study observes.[68]

LLATs are typically resistant to marrying again or being in a marriage-like relationship. But if marriage was once the only way we defined a romantic couple until cohabitation expanded that definition, how do we define a couple when they live separately, researchers studying LAT couples in France posit. "Perhaps we should abandon, at least temporarily, the idea that an indicator must be 'verified' or should be 'objective' and allow the individuals concerned to report themselves as 'non-cohabiting couples,' 'engaged in a serious unmarried intimate relationship' or in a 'relationship without ties.'"[314]

More couples, at least in the United States, are platonic couples. Writing in *The Atlantic*, Rhaina Cohen, author of 2024's *The Other Significant Others*, states that some people are prioritizing friendship over sexual-romantic relationships, sharing "many of the trappings of romantic relationships" such as buying houses together and having medical and legal powers of attorney for each other—just without having sex.[315]

It's similar to what many of the people who choose to live apart from their partners told sociologist and gender studies researcher Sasha Roseneil in her 2006 study: "Against the dominant heteronormative emphasis on finding and keeping a life-long conjugal partner, there was a widespread belief that such relationships are increasingly rare, and that a happier, more secure life is to be created by investing time and energy in maintaining friendships. This disinvesting in potentially risky sexual/love relationships and the prioritizing of friendships, which interviewees tended to regard as more stable and reliable, is an important part of the relational context within which lives were lived outside cohabiting relationships."[252]

In fact, she found that friends are often considered family for many LAT couples and an important source of support and care, including during times of illness.[316]

In his study of the future of LAT unions, University of Málaga sociologist Luis Ayuso observes that the lifestyle is more likely to find support in countries that are accepting of all forms of family life, not just married couples and the nuclear family, and among older, highly educated people. Those who live apart primarily as a way to maintain their independence generally don't expect to live together at some point, although it's not completely off the table. That, he says, highlights "the adaptability shown by these couples in their daily dynamics, as well as how elements such as communication within the couple are features that are increasingly more relevant than physical distance."[158]

Who would know that? Like I said, LAT relationships could use some good public relations.

Perhaps an aging world and the continued expansion of the many ways we are creating intimate relationships will enable more people to discover LAT relationships and help normalize it—one of the goals of this book. Will millennials, zoomers, Generation Alpha, and the generations to follow see their parents at some point embrace the LAT lifestyle? It wouldn't be surprising. Will they be inspired to consider it for themselves? Possibly.

"People haven't looked at alternative ways of being in relationships or being married. I like that it's coming out of the shadows," therapist and relationship expert Sherrie Sims Allen tells me. "The future is changing, how we relate to ourselves and other people."[119]

It is, thankfully, changing. You can be part of that change, whether you ultimately decide that it's a good fit for you or not. At least you can feel confident that you explored the possibility.

ENDNOTES

1. Wendy K. Watson and Stelle, Charlie. "Dating for Older Women: Experiences and Meanings of Dating in Later Life," *Journal of Women & Aging*, 2011, https://www.ncbi.nlm.nih.gov/pmc/articles/PMC4075761/#R7
2. Sofie Ghazanfareeon Karlsson and Borell, Klas, "Intimacy and Autonomy, Gender and Ageing: Living Apart Together," 27 *Aging International* 11, 14 (2002).
3. Wendy Lee, "People spend more time on mobile devices than TV, firm says," *Los Angeles Times*, June 5, 2019, accessed June 11, 2023, https://www.latimes.com/business/la-fi-ct-people-spend-more-time-on-mobile-than-tv-20190605-story.html
4. Nicole Pajer, "The Surprising Way Watching TV Can Make Your Relationship Stronger," *People*, Nov. 2, 2020, accessed June 11, 2023, https://people.com/lifestyle/want-to-stop-pandemic-fighting-with-your-partner-turn-on-the-tv/
5. Esther Perel, *The State of Affairs: Rethinking Infidelity* (New York, NY: Harper, 2017), 183
6. Gillian Anderson, "Gillian Anderson: 'Not Living Together Works so Well.'" *The Guardian*, Jan. 12, 2020. http://www.theguardian.com/culture/2020/jan/12/gillian-anderson-not-living-together-works-well-lat

7. Tammy La Gorce, "When a Love Expert Falls in Love," *The New York Times*, Aug. 21, 2020, http://www.nytimes.com/2020/08/21/fashion/weddings/when -a-love-expert-falls-in-love.html

8. See, e.g., Simon Duncan and Phillips, Miranda, "People Who Live Apart Together (LATs): New Family Form or Just a Stage?" *International Review of Sociology* 21, no. 3 (2011): 513–32, https://doi.org/10.1080/03906701.2011.6 25660; Arnaud Régnier-Loilier and Vignoli, Daniele, "The Diverse Nature of Living Apart Together Relationships: An Italy–France Comparison," *Journal of Population Research* 35, no. 1 (2018): 1–22, https://doi.org/10.1007/s12546 -017-9197-0); Anna Reimondos, Evans, Ann, and Gray, Edith, "Living-Apart -Together (LAT) Relationships in Australia," *Family Matters* 87, no. 43 (2011): 53, https://doi.org/https://melbourneinstitute.unimelb.edu.au/assets/documents /hilda-bibliography/conference-papers-lectures/2009/Reimondos_LAT_ TASA09.pdf; De Jong Gierveld, supra note 37, at 73–74; Caradec, supra note 52, at 906; Charles Q. Strohm et al., "'Living Apart Together' Relationships in the United States," 21 *Demographic Research* 177 (2009); https://www150. statcan.gc.ca/n1/pub/75-006-x/2013001/article/11771-eng.pdf

9. Simon Duncan et al., "Practices and Perceptions of Living Apart Together," *Family Science* 5, no. 1 (2014): 1–10, https://doi.org/10.1080/19424620.2014. 927382

10. bell hooks, "All About Love: New Visions" (New York, NY, HarperCollins Publishers, 2018), page 140

11. Stephanie Coontz, telephone conversation with author, Sept. 12, 2022.

12. Arielle Kuperberg. "Premarital Cohabitation and Direct Marriage in the United States: 1956–2015," *Marriage & Family Review*, 55:5 (2019), 447–475, doi: 10.1080/01494929.2018.1518820

13. Ronald R. Rindfuss and VandenHeuvel, Audrey. "Cohabitation: A Precursor to Marriage or an Alternative to Being Single?" *Population and Development Review* 16, no. 4 (1990): 703–26. https://doi.org/10.2307/1972963; Arielle Kuperberg (2019) "Premarital Cohabitation and Direct Marriage in the United States: 1956–2015," *Marriage & Family Review*, 55:5, 447-475, doi: 10.1080/01494929.2018.1518820

14. G. P. Murdock. *Social Structure* (New York, NY: Macmillan, 1949).

15. Stephanie Coontz, *Marriage: A History* (New York, NY: Penguin Books, 2006), page 26

16. Judith Stacey, *Unhitched: Love, Marriage, and Family Values from West Hollywood to Western China* (New York University Press, 2012), page 170

17. Tara Hunter, "Enslaved Couples Faced Wrenching Separations, or Even Choosing Family Over Freedom," History.com, Sept. 20, 2019, accessed Sept. 22, 2022, https://www.history.com/news/african-american-slavery-marriage-family-separation

18. John Koster, "Plural Wives and the Plains Indians," History.com, Aug. 16, 2017, accessed Sept. 22, 2022, https://www.historynet.com/plural-wives-plains-indians

19. Adee Braun, "The Once-Common Practice of Communal Sleeping," *Atlas Obscura*, June 22, 2017, accessed Sept. 22, 2022, https://www.atlasobscura.com/articles/communal-sleeping-history-sharing-bed

20. Wendy M. Troxel, "Is sleeping in separate beds bad for your relationship? A sleep scientist answers," Ideas TED, March 23, 2020, accessed Sept. 12, 2022, https://ideas.ted.com/is-sleeping-in-separate-beds-bad-for-your-relationship-a-sleep-scientist-answers

21. Juliana Menasce Horowitz, Graf, Nikki, and Livingston, Gretchen, "Why people get married or move in with a partner," Pew Research Center, Nov. 6, 2019, accessed Sept. 12, 2022, https://www.pewresearch.org/social-trends/2019/11/06/why-people-get-married-or-move-in-with-a-partner

22. Maria Brandén, Haandrikman, K. "Who Moves to Whom? Gender Differences in the Distance Moved to a Shared Residence." *Eur J Population* 35, 435–458 (2019). https://doi.org/10.1007/s10680-018-9490-4

23. Sandra Krapf, "Moving in or Breaking Up? The Role of Distance in the Development of Romantic Relationships." *Eur J Population* 34, 313–336 (2018). https://doi.org/10.1007/s10680-017-9428-2

24. Eli J. Finkel, *The All-Or-Nothing Marriage: How the Best Marriages Work* (New York, NY: Dutton, 2017), page 265.

25. Debra A. Neiman, telephone conversation with author, May 4, 2023.

26. Irene Levin and Trost, Jan. "Living Apart Together." *Community, Work & Family* 2 no. 3 (1999): 279–94

27. Irene Levin. "Living Apart Together: A New Family Form." *Current Sociology* 52 (2004): 223–240. 10.1177/0011392104041809

28. Karen Upton-Davis. "Living Apart Together Relationships (LAT): Severing Intimacy from Obligation." *Gender Issues*, September 2012. 25 38. 10.1007/s12147-012-9110-2.

29. Conference of European Statisticians' Task Force on Families and Households. 2009. Measurement of different emerging forms of households and families. http://www.unece.org/fileadmin/DAM/ stats/publications/Measurement_ermerging_forms_households_and_families.pdf

30. Esther Perel, *Mating in Captivity: Unlocking Erotic Intelligence* (New York, NY: HarperCollins, 2006), page 25.

31. Susan Pease Gadoua and Larson, Vicki, *The New I Do: Reshaping Marriage for Skeptics, Realists and Rebels* (New York, NY: Seal Press, 2014), pages 128–129.

32. "Aromantic-Spectrum Union for Recognition, Education, and Advocacy," AUREA, accessed Sept. 12, 2022, https://www.aromanticism.org

33. Andie Nordgren, "The short instructional manifesto for relationship anarchy," *The Anarchist Library,* July 14, 2012, accessed Sept. 12, 2022, https://theanarchistlibrary.org/library/andie-nordgren-the-short-instructional-manifesto-for-relationship-anarchy

34. Elizabeth Brake, *Minimizing Marriage: Marriage, Morality, and the Law* (Oxford University Press, 2012), page 5.

35. Mark S. Granovetter. "The Strength of Weak Ties." *American Journal of Sociology* 78, no. 6 (1973): 1360–80. http://www.jstor.org/stable/2776392; Volpe, Allie, "Why You Need a Network of Low-Stakes, Casual Friendships," *New York Times,* May 6, 2019, accessed Sept. 12, 2022, https://www,nytimes.com/2019/05/06/smarter-living/why-you-need-a-network-of-low-stakes-casual-friendships.html

36. Mallory Newall, "As pandemic drags on, relationships are getting more serious," Ipsos.com, Aug. 4, 2020, accessed Sept. 12, 2022, https://www.ipsos.com/en-us/news-polls/relationships-covid19

37. Birk Hagemeyer, Schönbrodt, F. D., Neyer, F. J., Neberich, W., and Asendorpf, J. B. "When 'Together' Means 'Too Close': Agency Motives and Relationship Functioning in Coresident and Living-Apart-Together Couples." *Journal of Personality and Social Psychology.* Advance online publication, Sept. 14, 2015. http://dx.doi.org/10.1037/pspi0000031

38. David Frost and Forrester, Cat. "Closeness Discrepancies in Romantic Relationships: Implications for Relational Well-Being, Stability, and Mental Health." *Personality & Social Psychology Bulletin* 39 (2013). 10.1177/0146167213476896

39. Mike Featherstone. *Consumer Culture and Postmodernism,* 1993, SAGE Publications Ltd. doi:10.4135/9781446288399

40. Sofie Ghazanfareeon Karlsson and Borell, Klas, "A Home of Their Own: Women's Boundary Work in LAT-Relationships," *Journal of Aging Studies* 19(1) 73, 74–75 (2005)

41. Jochen Hirschle, "Reorganizing social life after separation," paper presented at the European Network for the Sociological & Demographic Study of Divorce,

Oxford, Oct. 26–28, 2013, http://cv- jh.com/Hirschle_SeparationConsequences_Oxford2013.pdf

42. Kirsten Gram-Hanssen, and Bech-Danielsen, Claus. "Home dissolution: What happens after separation?" *Housing Studies*, 23 no. 3 (2008), 507–522.

43. Júlia Mikolai, Kulu, Hill, Mulder, Clara H. "Family life transitions, residential relocations, and housing in the life course: Current research and opportunities for future work: Introduction to the Special Collection on 'Separation, Divorce, and Residential Mobility in a Comparative Perspective,'" *Demographic Research*, 10.4054/DemRes.2020.43.2, 43, (35-58), 2020.

44. Harriet Young and Grundy, Emily. "Living arrangements, health and well-being" in John Stillwell, Ernestina Coast, and Dylan Kneale, editors, *Fertility, living arrangements, care and mobility*, volume 1 of Understanding Population Trends and Processes, chapter 7, pages 127–150. Springer, 2009.

45. Kirsty Kawano, "Graduating from Marriage, the Japanese Phenomenon of Sotsukon," Feb. 5, 2020, accessed Nov. 13, 2022, https://savvytokyo.com/graduating-from-marriage-the-japanese-phenomenon-of-sotsukon

46. Elizabeth Bernstein, "Need Space in a Relationship? Just Don't Say It That Way," *The Wall Street Journal*, June 26, 2012, accessed Nov. 13, 2022, https://www.wsj.com/articles/SB10001424052702303836404577474460720719018

47. Suzanne Bianchi, Robinson, John and Milke, Melissa. *The Changing Rhythms of American Family Life* (New York, NY: Russell, 2006).

48. Karen Upton-Davis. "Subverting gendered norms of cohabitation: Living Apart Together for women over 45," *Journal of Gender Studies*, 24:1 (2015), 104–116, doi: 10.1080/09589236.2013.861346

49. Samantha Joel, "Living Apart, Together: Why Some Couples are Forgoing Cohabitation," *Luvze*, Oct. 23, 2013, accessed Nov. 13, 2022, https://www.luvze.com/living-apart-together-why-some-couples-are-forgoing-cohabita/

50. Dietrich Klusmann. 2002. "Sexual motivation and duration of partnership." *Archives of Sexual Behavior* 31. 275 87.10.1023/A:1015205020769

51. Cynthia Graham, Mercer, Catherine, Tanton, Clare, et al. "What factors are associated with reporting lacking interest in sex and how do these vary by gender? Findings from the third British national survey of sexual attitudes and lifestyles," *BMJ Open* 2017;7:e016942. doi: 10.1136/bmjopen-2017-016942

52. Daniel Bergner, "Unexcited? There May Be a Pill for That," *The New York Times*, May 22, 2013, accessed Nov. 13, 2022, https://www.nytimes.com/2013/05/26/magazine/unexcited-there-may-be-a-pill-for-that.html

53. Ali Ziegler, Matsick, Jes L., Moors, Amy C., Rubin, Jennifer D., and Conley,

Terri D. 2012. "Does Monogamy Harm Women? Deconstructing Monogamy With a Feminist Lens." *Journal für Psychologie* 22 (1). https://journal- fuerpsychologie.de/article/view/323

54. Kristen Mark, Rosenkrantz, Dani, Kerner, Ian. 2014. "'Bi'ing into monogamy: Attitudes toward monogamy in a sample of bisexual-identified adults." *Psychology of Sexual Orientation and Gender Diversity*, 1, 263–269. http://dx.doi.org/10.1037/sgd0000051

55. Karen Kobayashi, Funk, Laura, and Khan, Mushira Mohsin. "Constructing a Sense of Commitment in 'Living Apart Together' (LAT) Relationships: Interpretive Agency and Individualization." *Current Sociology* 65, no. 7 (November 2017): 991–1009. https://doi.org/10.1177/0011392116653237

56. Benjamin Le, Korn, Miriam S., Crockett, Erin E., and Loving, Timothy J. 2011. "Missing you maintains us: Missing a romantic partner, commitment, relationship maintenance, and physical infidelity." *Journal of Social and Personal Relationships* 28, 653-667; Le, B., Loving, T. J., Lewandowski, G. W. Jr., Feinberg, E. G., Johnson, K. C., Fiorentino, R., and Ing, J. (2008). "Missing a romantic partner: A prototype analysis." *Personal Relationships* 15, 511–532

57. Eva Illouz, *Why Love Hurts: A Sociological Explanation* (Cambridge, U.K., Polity Press, March 2012).

58. Matthew D. Johnson, Lavner, Justin A., Mund, Marcus, Zemp, Martina, Stanley, Scott M., Neyer, Franz J., Impett, Emily A., et al. "Within-Couple Associations Between Communication and Relationship Satisfaction Over Time." *Personality and Social Psychology Bulletin* 48, no. 4 (April 2022): 534–49. https://doi.org/10.1177/01461672211016920.

59. Sara Mietzner and Li-Wen, Lin. "Would you do it again? Relationship skills gained in a long-distance relationship." *College Student Journal*, vol. 39, no. 1 (March 2005), pp. 192+. Gale Academic OneFile, link.gale.com/apps/doc/A131318259/AONE?u=anon~cc2ec02d&sid=googleScholar&xid=7cb481b7. Accessed Aug. 29, 2022.

60. Gretchen Kelmer et al., "Relationship Quality, Commitment, and Stability in Long-Distance Relationships," *Family Process* 52, no. 2 (Sept. 18, 2012), https://doi.org/10.1111/j.1545-5300.2012.01418.x.

61. Scott M. Stanley, Kline Rhoades, Galena, and Markman, Howard J. 2006. "Sliding versus deciding: Inertia and the premarital cohabitation effect." *Family Relations* 55, 499-509

62. Julia Carter. 2012. "What is commitment? Women's accounts of intimate attachment." *Families, Relationships and Societies* 1 (2). pp. 137–153.

63. Susan Pease Gadoua and Larson, Vicki. *The New I Do: Reshaping Marriage for Skeptics, Realists and Rebels* (New York, NY: Seal Press, 2014), pages 129–130.
64. GSS 1972-2021 Cumulative Datafile, DocDroid, https://www.docdroid.net/Mjb1sav/tables-sda7-pdf; accessed Nov. 13, 2022
65. Kristen Bialik, "Americans unhappy with family, social or financial life are more likely to say they feel lonely," Pew Research Center, Dec. 3, 2018, accessed Nov. 13, 2022, https://www.pewresearch.org/short-reads/2018/12/03/americans-unhappy-with-family-social-or-financial-life-are-more-likely-to-say-they-feel-lonely/
66. GSS Data Explorer | NORC at the University of Chicago, GSS Data Explorer, NORC at the University of Chicago, accessed Nov. 13, 2022, https://gssdataexplorer.norc.org/trends.
67. Simon Duncan, "Why more couples are choosing to live apart," *The Conversation*, Jan. 3, 2023, accessed Nov. 13, 2022, https://theconversation.com/why-more-couples-are-choosing-to-live-apart-124532
68. Ingrid Arnet Connidis, Borell, Klas, and Ghazanfareeon Karlsson, Sofie. "Ambivalence and Living Apart Together in Later Life: A Critical Research Proposal." *Journal of Marriage and Family* 79 (2017): 1404–1418. https://doi.org/10.1111/jomf.12417
69. Simon Duncan. "Women's Agency in Living Apart Together: Constraint, Strategy and Vulnerability." *The Sociological Review* 63, no. 3 (August 2015): 589–607. https://doi.org/10.1111/1467-954X.12184
70. Sofie Ghazanfareeon Karlsson, and Borell, Klas. "Intimacy and autonomy, gender and ageing: Living apart together." *Ageing Int.* 27, 11–26 (2002). https://doi.org/10.1007/s12126-002-1012-2 at 18-19; Ofra Or. "Midlife Women in Second Partnerships Choosing Living Apart Together: An Israeli Case Study." *Israel Studies Review* 28, no. 2 (2013): 41–60. http://www.jstor.org/stable/43771862 at 46
71. Ofra Or. "Midlife Women in Second Partnerships Choosing Living Apart Together: An Israeli Case Study." *Israel Studies Review* 28, no. 2 (2013): 41–60. http://www.jstor.org/stable/43771862 at 46
72. Roselinde Van der Wiel, Mulder, Clara H., Bailey, Ajay. "Pathways to commitment in living-apart-together relationships in the Netherlands: A study on satisfaction, alternatives, investments and social support." *Advances in Life Course Research*, 36 (2018), 13–22. https://doi.org/10.1016/j.alcr.2018.03.001
73. Alisa C. Lewin. "Health and relationship quality later in life: A comparison

of living apart together (LAT), first marriages, remarriages, and cohabitation." *Journal of Family Issues*, 38 no. 12 (2017), 1754–1774. https://doi.org/10.1177/0192513X16647982

74. Tusi-o Tai, Baxter, Janeen, Hewitt, Belinda, "Do coresidence and intentions make a difference? Relationship satisfaction in married, cohabiting, and living apart together couples in four countries." *Demographic Research*, 19 (3) (2014), pp. 71–104

75. Laura M. Funk and Kobayashi, Karen M. "From motivations to accounts: an interpretive analysis of 'Living Apart Together' relationships in mid- to late-life." Journal of Family Issues, 37 no. 8 (2016), 1101–1122. doi: 10.1177/0192513X14529432; Ryan Flanagan. "Together, but apart: 1.5 million Canadians living away from their partners," CTV News, Feb. 20, 2019, accessed Nov. 13, 2022, https://www.ctvnews.ca/lifestyle/together-but-apart-1-5-million-canadians-living-away-from-their-partners

76. Zosia Bielski, "The new reality of dating over 65: Men want to live together; women don't," *The Globe and Mail*, Nov. 22, 2022, accessed Jan. 13, 2022, theglobeandmail.com/life/relationships/article-women-older-than-65-dont-want-to-live-with-their-partners

77. "'Don't trade your pension for a prostate.' Readers react to the reality of dating over 65 and women who don't want to live together," *The Globe and Mail*, Nov. 30, 2019, accessed Jan. 13, 2022, https://www.theglobeandmail.com/canada/article-dont-trade-your-pension-for-a-prostate-readers-react-to-the/

78. Huijing Wu and Brown, Susan L. "Union Formation Expectations Among Older Adults Who Live Apart Together in the USA." *Journal of Family Issues* (July 2021). https://doi.org/10.1177/0192513X211031518

79. Denis Brothers. "'Doing' LAT: Redoing gender and family in living apart together relationships in later life." *Innovation in Aging*, 1 (Suppl 1), (2017), 820. https://doi.org/10.1093/geroni/igx004.2960

80. Chaya Koren. "The intertwining of second couplehood and old age." *Ageing and Society*, 35 (2015), 1864–1888

81. Terri Langford, and Rudner, Jordan, "Supreme Court Justice Antonin Scalia Found Dead in West Texas," *Texas Tribune*, Feb. 13, 2016, accessed Sept. 12, 2022, https://www.texastribune.org/2016/02/13/us-supreme-court-justice-antonin-scalia-found-dead

82. Bella DePaulo, "The Ultimate Threat to Single People: You'll Die Alone," *Psychology Today*, Jan. 23, 2009, accessed Sept. 12, 2022, https://www.psychologytoday.com/us/blog/living-single/200901/the-ultimate-threat-single-people

-youll-die-alone

83. Jamie Wheal, host. "Helen Fischer, PhD," *Homegrown Humans* (podcast), Jan. 7, 2021, accessed Jan. 14, 2023, https://neurohacker.com/homegrown -humans-helen-fisher-ph-d-sexuality-hosted-by-jamie-wheal-podcast

84. Roxanne Roberts, "At 81, Diane Rehm is again a blushing bride," *The Florida Times Union*–Jacksonville.com, Oct. 15, 2017, accessed Jan. 14, 2023, https:// www.jacksonville.com/story/news/nation-world/2017/10/16/81-diane-rehm -again-blushing-bride/16291086007/

85. Alison Brody, "A Note From Diane On Her Upcoming Marriage," Diane Rehm blog, Oct. 11, 2017, accessed Jan. 14, 2023 https://dianerehm.org/2017/10/11 /a-note-from-diane-on-her-upcoming-marriage

86. Laura Stassi, host. "Custom-Built Commitment," *Dating While Gray* (podcast), April 2, 2020, accessed Jan. 14, 2023, https://wamu.org/story/20/04/02 /custom-built-commitment

87. Dara Klatt, "My Washington: Diane Rehm," *Washington Life Magazine*, Feb. 13, 2020, accessed Jan. 14, 2023, https://washingtonlife.com/2020/02/13 /my-washington-diane-rehm/

88. Joyce Maynard, Facebook post, Sept. 14, 2022, accessed Jan. 14, 2023, https:// www.facebook.com/photo?fbid=628282878666092&set=a.274669610694 089

89. Sofie Ghazanfareeon Karlsson, and Borell, Klas. "A home of their own: Women's boundary work in LAT-relationship." *Journal of Aging Studies*. (2005). 73–84. 10.1016/j.jaging.2004.03.008.

90. Laura Stassi, *Romance Redux: Finding Love in Your Later Years* (Lanham, Md.: Rowman & Littlefield Publishers, 2022) page 127

91. Cynthia Grant Bowman, *Living Apart Together: Legal Protections for a New Family Form* (New York University Press, 2020) page 67.

92. David Eichert. "Gay Male Couples and LAT." In *Living Apart Together* (New York University Press, 2020). https://doi.org/10.18574 /nyu/9781479891047.003.0006, page 78–96.

93. Ibid, 86.

94. Ibid, 87.

95. Charles Strohm, Seltzer, Judith, Cochran, Susan, and Mays, Vickie. "'Living Apart Together': Relationships in the United States." *Demographic Research* 21 (Aug. 13, 2009): 177–214. doi:10.4054/demres.2009.21.7

96. Jessica Klein, "Does 'solo polyamory' mean having it all?" BBC.com, March 4, 2022, accessed Jan. 14, 2023, https://www.bbc.com/worklife

/article/20220301-does-solo-polyamory-mean-having-it-all

97. Ike Allen, "Diego Rivera and Frida Kahlo House Studio Museum," *Atlas Obscura*, June 30, 2017, accessed Jan. 14, 2023, https://www.atlasobscura.com/places/museo-casa-estudio-diego-rivera-y-frida-kahlo

98. Joseph Harry. "The 'Marital' Liaisons of Gay Men." *The Family Coordinator* 28, no. 4 (1979): 622–29. https://doi.org/10.2307/583527

99. Chateau de Versailles, "The Queen's Apartments," accessed Jan. 14, 2023, https://en.chateauversailles.fr/discover/estate/palace/queen-apartments

100. Owen Jarus, "Palace of Versailles: Facts & History," *Live Science*, Oct. 4, 2017, accessed Sept. 19, 2022, https://www.livescience.com/38903-palace-of-versailles-facts-history.html

101. Reddit, accessed Sept. 23, 2022, https://www.reddit.com/r/NeurodiverseCouples/comments/t1cry4/comment/i1uf15e/?utm_source=share&utm_medium=web2x&context=3

102. Disability Rights Education & Defense Fund, "Marriage Equality," accessed Dec. 12, 2022, https://dredf.org/marriage-equality

103. "Scandinavia Living Apart Together," *Marriage: Cultural Aspects*, Marriage and Family Encyclopedia, accessed March 19, 2023, https://family.jrank.org/pages/1452/Scandinavia-Living-Apart-Together.html; Ingrid Arnet Connidis, Borell, Klas, and Karlsson, Sofie Ghazanfareeon, "Ambivalence and Living Apart Together in Later Life: A Critical Research Proposal." *Journal of Marriage and Family* 79 (2017): 1404–1418. https://doi.org/10.1111/jomf.12417

104. Yun-Suk Lee. "Weekend Couples as a Manifestation of Gender Equality?" *Asian Journal of Social Science* 48, (2020) 3–4: 294–318, doi: https://doi.org/10.1163/15685314-04803006; Yun-Suk Lee. "Marital Satisfaction among Korean Commuter Couples." *Asian Journal of Social Science* 46 (2018): 182–203.

105. Clare Ansberry, "The Secret to These Successful Marriages? Living Apart," *The Wall Street Journal*, Dec. 5, 2021, accessed Sept. 25, 2022, https://www.wsj.com/articles/the-secret-to-these-successful-marriages-living-apart-11638716401

106. James Barron, "Not Sleeping Enough? Arianna Huffington Wants to Help," *The New York Times*, Dec. 4, 2016, accessed Sept. 26, 2022, https://www.nytimes.com/2016/12/04/nyregion/not-sleeping-enough-arianna-huffington-wants-to-help.html

107. Paul Raeburn, "Arianna Huffington: Collapse from exhaustion was 'wake-up call," *Today*, May 9, 2014, accessed Sept. 26, 2022, https://www.today.com/health/arianna-huffington-collapse-exhaustion-was-wake-call-2D79644042

108. Ariana Huffington, *The Sleep Revolution: Transforming Your Life, One Night at a Time* (New York, NY: Harmony, 2017); Reprint edition, page 196.

109. Quora, "Sleep Tips And Strategies To Get A Good Night's Sleep From Arianna Huffington," *Forbes,* May 10, 2016, accessed Sept. 26, 2022, https://www. forbes.com/sites/quora/2016/05/10/sleep-tips-and-strategies-to-get-a-good -nights-sleep-from-arianna-huffington/?sh=53fb0adf2d0c

110. Daryl Austin, "For Couples, Sleeping Apart Actually Could Have Health Benefits," *The Washington Post,* Aug. 7, 2021, accessed Sept. 26, 2022, https://www.washingtonpost.com/health/sleeping-problem-separate -beds/2021/08/06/61340332-e800-11eb-ba5d-55d3b5ffcaf1_story.html

111. Meredith E. Rumble, Okoyeh, Paul, and Benca, Ruth M., "Sleep and Women's Mental Health," Psychiatric Clinics of North America, May 27, 2023, https:// doi.org/10.1016/j.psc.2023.04.008

112. Alyssa Giacobbe, "This Is the Hottest New Amenity in Luxury Homes," *Architectural Digest,* March 27, 2017, accessed Oct. 2, 2022, https://www. architecturaldigest.com/story/dual-master-suites-in-luxury-homes

113. Judye Hess and Catell, Padma, "Dual Dwelling Duos," *Journal of Couples Therapy*, 10:3–4, (2001): 25–31, doi: 10.1300/J036v10n03_04

114. Laura Stassl, host. "The Parent Trap," *Dating While Gray* (podcast), Nov. 16, 2022, accessed Nov. 27, 2022, https://www.wunc.org/2022-11-16/transcript -the-parent-trap

115. A. W. Geiger and Livingston, Gretchen, "8 facts about love and marriage in America," Pew Research Center, Feb. 13, 2019, accessed April 7, 2023, https:// www.pewresearch.org/fact-tank/2019/02/13/8-facts-about-love-and-marriage

116. Deborah A. Widiss. "Changing the Marriage Equation," *Washington University Law Review* 89 (2012). 721 https://openscholarship.wustl.edu/law _lawreview/vol89/iss4/1

117. Kasey J. Eickmeyer, and Manning, Wendy D. "Serial Cohabitation in Young Adulthood: Baby Boomers to Millennials." *Journal of Marriage and Family* 80 (4). (August 2018): 826–840. doi: 10.1111/jomf.12495

118. Arnaud Régnier-Loilier and Vignoli, Daniele. "The Diverse Nature of Living Apart Together Relationships: An Italy-France Comparison." *Journal of Population Research* 35, no. 1 (2018): 1–22. http://www.jstor.org/stable/45179130

119. Sherrie Sims Allen, telephone conversation with author, Jan. 13, 2023.

120. Benjamin Le, Korn, Miriam S., Crockett, Erin E., and Loving, Timothy J. "Missing you maintains us: Missing a romantic partner, commitment, relationship maintenance, and physical infidelity." *Journal of Social and Personal*

Relationships 28 no. 5 (2011) 653–667.

121. Eva Illouz, *Why Love Hurts: A Sociological Explanation* (New York, NY: Polity, 2013), page 114.

122. Heather "Lulu" Mazzei, telephone conversation with author, Aug. 19, 2022.

123. Elaine Romero, telephone conversation with author, Nov. 11, 2022.

124. Betsy Hart, "'Living apart together' relationship ultimately selfish," *Deseret News*, May 13, 2006, accessed Nov. 18, 2022, https://www.deseret.com/2006/5/14/19952920/living-apart-together-relationship-ultimately-selfish

125. Bella DePaulo, "Unselfish Singles: They Give More Time, Money, and Care," *Psychology Today*, Feb. 24, 2017, accessed Nov. 20, 2022, https://www.psychologytoday.com/us/blog/living-single/201702/unselfish-singles-they-give-more-time-money-and-care

126. Bella DePaulo, "What Singles Share with Couples Who Do Not Want to Marry or Even Live Together," *Medium*, Dec. 2, 2020, accessed Nov. 20, 2022, https://medium.com/fourth-wave/what-singles-share-with-couples-who-do-not-want-to-marry-or-even-live-together-3fbc338e79b7

127. Audrey R. Giles and Oncescu, Jacquelyn. "Single Women's Leisure During the Coronavirus Pandemic," *Leisure Sciences*, 43:1-2 (2021), 204–210, doi: 10.1080/01490400.2020.1774003

128. Mara A. Yerkes, Roeters, Anne, and Baxter, Janeen. "Gender differences in the quality of leisure: a cross-national comparison," *Community, Work & Family* 23:4 (2020), 367–384, doi: 10.1080/13668803.2018.1528968

129. Bowman, *Living Apart Together: Legal Protections for a New Form of Family*, 106–107.

130. Bella DePaulo, *How We Live Now: Redefining Home and Family in the 21st Century* (Portland, Ore:, Atria Books/Beyond Words, Aug. 25, 2015), page 181.

131. Sharon Hyman, "We've been together 23 years and never lived together. Here's why it works," *Today*, Dec. 16, 2021, accessed Oct. 14, 2022, https://www.today.com/health/essay/living-apart-together-sharon-hyman-relationship-rcna8781

132. Simon Duncan and Phillips, Miranda. "People who live apart together (LATs)—how different are they?" *The Sociological Review* 58 (2010), 112–134.

133. Rachel Paula Abrahamson, "Van Jones welcomes baby girl with long-time friend as 'conscious co-parents,'" *Today*, Feb. 14, 2022, accessed Nov. 26, 2022, https://www.today.com/parents/dads/van-jones-baby-girl-longtime-friend-conscious-co-parents-rcna16186

134. "Living Apart, Parenting Together: Collaborating with your Coparent," *Zero*

to Three, May 3, 2018, accessed Nov. 26, 2022, https://www.zerotothree.org /resource/living-apart-parenting-together-collaborating-with-your-coparent

135. Tullia Jack, Ivanova, Diana, Buchs, Milena, and Gram-Hanssen, Kirsten, "Why more people than ever are living alone—and what this means for the environment," *The Conversation*, March 3, 2021, accessed Dec. 25, 2022, https://theconversation.com/why-more-people-than-ever-are-living-alone-and -what-this-means-for-the-environment-156328

136. Daisy Meager, "All the Ways Restaurants Ruin the Environment," *Vice*, Feb. 25, 2019, accessed Jan. 4, 2023, https://www.vice.com/en/article/8xyvpb/all -the-ways-restaurants-ruin-the-environment

137. Lukas Kala. "The Environmental Impact of Singles' Consumer Behaviour: Is the Lifestyle of Singles Inevitably Environmentally More Damaging?" *Sociální studia* 12 (2015). 53–69. 10.5817/SOC2015-3-53

138. Diane Rehm, email with author, Oct. 4, 2022.

139. Jacky Vallée, email with author, Oct. 4, 2022. 140. Constance Rosenblum, "Living Apart Together," *The New York Times*, Sept. 13, 2013, accessed Oct. 1, 2022, https://www.nytimes.com/2013/09/15/realestate/living-apart -together.html

141. Mariya Stoilova, Roseneil, Sasha, Crowhurst, Isabel, Hellesund, Tone, and Santos, Ana Cristina. "Living Apart Relationships in Contemporary Europe: Accounts of Togetherness and Apartness." *Sociology* 48(6), (2014): 1075–1091. https://doi.org/10.1177/0038038514523697

142. Kate Bolick, "Divide and Conquer: Married Couples Living Apart," *Elle*, March 4, 2012, accessed Jan. 30, 2023, https://www.elle.com/life-love/sex -relationships/advice/a11889/divide-conquer-married-but-separate-644331

143. Bernadette Bawin-Legros, and Gauthier, Anne. "Regulation of Intimacy and Love Semantics in Couples Living Apart Together," *International Review of Sociology* 11:1, (2001): 39–46, doi:10.1080/03906700020030983

144. Orna Donath, Berkovitch, Nitza, and Segal-Engelchin, Dorit, "'I Kind of Want to Want': Women Who Are Undecided About Becoming Mothers." *Frontiers in Psychology* 13 (2022) 848384, https://doi.org/10.3389/fpsyg.2022.848384

145. Ruddy Faure, McNulty, James K., Meltzer, Andrea L., and Righetti, Francesca. "Implicit Ambivalence: A Driving Force to Improve Relationship Problems." *Social Psychological and Personality Science* 13(2), (2022): 500–511. https:// doi.org/10.1177/19485506211034277

146. Elizabeth Pleck, *Not Just Roommates: Cohabitation after the Sexual Revolution* (University of Chicago Press, 2012), page 47.

147. Madeleine Schwartz, "One marriage under god," *Salon*, Feb. 2, 2013, accessed Oct. 10, 2022, https://www.salon.com/2013/02/02/one_marriage_under_god

148. Penelope M. Huang et al., "He Says, She Says: Gender and Cohabitation," *Journal of Family Issues* 32, no. 7 (Feb. 3, 2011), https://doi.org /10.1177/0192513x10397601

149. Lise Stoessel, phone conversation with author, Feb. 13, 2023.

150. Lise Stoessel, *Living Happily Ever After—Separately: How Separate Spaces Could Save Your Marriage* (Richmond, Va., Brandylane Publishers, Inc., 2011), page 29.

151. Anna Sale, *Let's Talk About Hard Things: The Life-Changing Conversations That Connect Us* (New York, NY: Simon & Schuster, 2022), page 13.

152. Amy R. Overton and Lowry, Ann C. "Conflict management: difficult conversations with difficult people," *Clinics in Colon and Rectal Surgery*. 2013; 26(4):259–64. doi:10.1055/s-0033-1356728

153. Sale, *Let's Talk About Hard Things*, page 10.

154. Hallie Levine, "My Husband and I Are Happily Married—And We Live Apart," *Prevention*, April 7, 2016, accessed Oct. 1, 2022, https://www. prevention.com/sex/a20507154/married-and-living-apart/

155. Susan Pease Gadoua, phone conversation with author, Dec. 5, 2022.

156. Catherine Hodder, "How To Live Apart Together and Avoid Legal Hurdles," *FindLaw*, Feb. 21, 2023, accessed March 11, 2023. https://www.findlaw.com /legalblogs/law-and-life/how-to-live-apart-together-and-avoid-legal-hurdles/

157. Frank Bruni, "Of Love and Fungus," *The New York Times*, July 20, 2013, accessed Nov. 21, 2022, https://www.nytimes.com/2013/07/21/opinion /sunday/bruni-of-love-and-fungus.html

158. Luis Ayuso. "What future awaits couples Living Apart Together (LAT)?" *The Sociological Review* 67 (2018). 003802611879905. 10.1177/0038026118799053.

159. Elaine and Abe Romero, hosts. "Top Things To Never Say." *Love Is in the Air* (podcast), Nov. 16, 2020, accessed Oct. 17, 2022, https://www.spreaker.com /user/13500687/1-top-things-to-never-say

160. Judye Hess, phone conversation with author, Dec. 5, 2022.

161. Dana Che, host, "Commuter Marriage: How Absence Makes the Heart Grow Fonder—with Abe and Elaine Romero," *Real Relationship Talk* (podcast), March 9, 2021, accessed Oct. 17, 2022, https://realrelationshiptalk.com /30-commuter-marriage-how-absence-makes-the-heart-grow-fonder-with -abe-and-elaine-romero

162. Ili Rivera Walter, phone conversation with author, March 24, 2023.

163. E. A. Marconi, email exchange with author, Aug. 6, 2022.

164. Rachel Shatto, "This Is When You Know You're Ready to Give Your Partner a Key, According to Experts," *Elite Daily*, July 20, 2018, accessed Feb. 6, 2023, https://www.elitedaily.com/p/should-you-give-your-partner-a-key-heres-what-experts-say-since-this-is-a-big-step-9820219

165. Vicki Hoefle, *Parenting as Partners: How to Launch Your Kids Without Ejecting Your Spouse* (Milton Park, Abingdon, Oxfordshire, U.K.: Routledge, 2017), page 21.

166. Wendy M. Troxel, phone conversation with author, April 19, 2023.

167. Amy Rauer, Sabey, Allen K., Proulx, Christine M., Volling, Brenda L. "What Are the Marital Problems of Happy Couples? A Multimethod, Two Sample Investigation," *Family Process*, 2019; doi: 10.1111/famp.12483

168. "Survey: Certified Divorce Financial Analyst® (CDFA®) Professionals Reveal the Leading Causes of Divorce," The Institute for Divorce Financial Analysts, accessed Feb. 3, 2023, https://institutedfa.com/Leading-Causes-Divorce

169. J. P. Dew. "Revisiting financial issues and marriage." In J. J. Xiao (Ed.), *Handbook of Consumer Finance Research*, 2nd Ed (pp. 281–290). (New York, NY: Springer, 2016).

170. Fran Bennett. "Researching Within-Household Distribution: Overview, Developments, Debates, and Methodological Challenges." *Journal of Marriage and Family* 75, no. 3 (2013): pages 582–597. http://www.jstor.org/stable/23440902

171. K. L. Archuleta. "Couples, money, and expectations: Negotiating financial management roles to increase relationship satisfaction." *Marriage and Family Review* 49(5), (2013): 391–411. https://doi.org/10.1080/01494929.2013.766296

172. "Making cents of love & money: 64% of coupled consumers admit to financial incompatibility with their partners," Bread Financial, Feb. 1, 2023, accessed May 8, 2032, https://newsroom.breadfinancial.com/making-cents-of-love-and-money

173. Megan McCoy, White, K. J., and Chen, X. "Exploring How One's Primary Financial Conversant Varies by Marital Status." *Journal of Financial Therapy* 10 (2) 3 (2019). https://doi.org/10.4148/1944-9771.1193; Megan McCoy email with author, May 9, 2023.

174. Sofie Ghazanfareeon Karlsson and Borell, Klas. "Intimacy and autonomy, gender and ageing: Living apart together." *Ageing International* 27. (2002): 11–26. 10.1007/s12126-002-1012-2

175. Lars Evertsson and Nyman, Charlott. "Perceptions and practices in

independent management: Blurring the boundaries between 'mine,' 'yours' and 'ours.'" *Journal of Family and Economic Issues* 35(1) (2014): 65–80, https://doi.org/10.1007/s10834-012-9348-6

176. Fenaba R. Addo. "Financial Integration and Relationship Transitions of Young Adult Cohabiters." *Journal of Family and Economic Issues* 38(1), (2017): 84–99. PMCID: PMC6049089, https://doi.org/10.1007/s10834-016-9490-7

177. Vicky Lyssens-Danneboom and Mortelmans, Dimitri. "Living Apart Together and Money: New Partnerships, Traditional Gender Roles." *Journal of Marriage and Family* 76, no. 5 (2014): 949–66. doi:10.1111/JOMF.12136

178. Rachel Clark, email with author, Oct. 6, 2022.

179. Beverly Harzog, "Survey: Nearly a Third Have Experienced Financial Infidelity," *U.S. News & World Report*, Jan. 18, 2023, accessed May 6, 2023, https://money.usnews.com/credit-cards/articles/survey-nearly-a-third-have-experienced-financial-infidelity

180. T. M. Jensen, Shafer, K., Guo, S., and Larson, J. H. "Differences in Relationship Stability Between Individuals in First and Second Marriages: A Propensity Score Analysis." *Journal of Family Issues* 38(3), (2017): 406–432, https://journals.sagepub.com/doi/10.1177/0192513X15604344

181. Richard L. Kaplan, "Preferencing Nonmarriage in Later Years." University of Illinois College of Law Legal Studies Research Paper No. 22-33, Forthcoming, *Washington University Law Review*, Vol. 99, No. 6 (Aug. 15, 2022) pp. 1957–82, https://ssrn.com/abstract=4190570

182. "Cost of Care Survey," Genworth, accessed May 8, 2023, https://www.genworth.com/aging-and-you/finances/cost-of-care.html

183. Richard Kaplan, email with author, May 9, 2023.

184. Kate Ashford, "Your house or mine: The life of couples who live apart," BBC Worklife, Aug. 9, 2015, accessed March 25, 2023, https://www.bbc.com/worklife/article/20150807-your-house-or-mine

185. Internal Revenue Service. (2014). Publication 501, accessed May 13, 2023, http://www.irs.gov/publications/p501/ar02.html

186. "Can I Claim a Boyfriend/Girlfriend as a Dependent on Income Taxes?" Intuit TurboTax, April 11, 2023, accessed May 13, 2023, https://turbotax.intuit.com/tax-tips/family/can-i-claim-a-boyfriend-girlfriend-as-a-dependent-on-income-taxes-/L12RRXt6j

187. Alexander Gattig and Minkus, Lara. "Does Marriage Increase Couples' Life Satisfaction? Evidence Using Panel Data and Fixed-Effects Individual Slopes." *Comparative Population Studies* 46 (May 2021). Wiesbaden, Germany. https://

doi.org/10.12765/CPoS-2021-05

188. Sarah O'Brien, "Remarried after having kids? Here are tips to avoid accidentally disinheriting them," CNBC, Jan. 17, 2019, accessed May 5, 2023, https://www.cnbc.com/2019/01/17/estate-planning-for-second-marriages-when-you-have-kids.html

189. Jenny de Jong Gierveld, and Merz, Eva-Maria. "Parents' Partnership Decision Making After Divorce or Widowhood: The Role of (Step)Children." *Journal of Marriage and Family* 75, no. 5 (2013): 1098–1113. http://www.jstor.org/stable/24583360

190. Susan B. Sorenson and Spear, Devan, "New Data on Intimate Partner Violence and Intimate Relationships: Implications for Gun Laws and Federal Data Collection," *Preventive Medicine* 107 (2018): 103–108.

191. "What is the 'boyfriend loophole'?" Everytown for Gun Safety, July 29, 2020, accessed Dec. 3, 2022, https://www.everytown.org/what-is-the-boyfriend-loophole

192. Nancy Leong, "Negative Identity," 88 *Southern California Law Review* 1357 (Aug. 22, 2014). U Denver Legal Studies Research Paper No. 14-55, https://ssrn.com/abstract=2485156

193. W. L. Morris, Sinclair, S., and DePaulo, B. M. "No shelter for singles: The perceived legitimacy of marital status discrimination." *Group Processes & Intergroup Relations*, 10(4), (2007): 457–470. https://doi.org/10.1177/1368430207081535

194. Ayesha Elaine Lewis, phone conversation with author, Dec. 12, 2022.

195. Sasha Roseneil, Crowhurst, Isabel, Hellesund, Tone, Santos, Ana Cristina, and Stoilova, Mariya. *The Tenacity of the Couple-Norm: Intimate Citizenship Regimes in a Changing Europe* (London: UCL Press, 2020), https://doi.org/10.2307/j.ctv13xpsd5

196. Pilar Wiegand Cruz, "The changing social gradient of marriage and cohabitation in seven Latin American countries," *Social Science Research*, Volume 113, 2023, 102898, ISSN 0049-089X, https://doi.org/10.1016/j.ssresearch.2023.102898

197. Carmen Diana Deere and León, Magdalena. "Consensual unions, property rights, and patrimonial violence against women in Latin America." *Social Politics: International Studies in Gender, State & Society* 29, no. 2 (2022): 608–633

198. Carol McGrath, "How couples living in separate homes say they have more success at love," *Global News*, March 12, 2022, accessed March 19, 2023,

https://globalnews.ca/news/8675443/couples-living-apart-together/

199. Bowman, *Living Apart Together: Legal Protections for a New Form of Family*, 162.

200. Susan Pease Gadoua and Larson, Vicki, *The New I Do: Reshaping Marriage for Skeptics, Realists and Rebels* (New York, NY: Seal Press, 2014), page 216.

201. Bowman, *Living Apart Together: Legal Protections for a New Form of Family*, 160.

202. Simon Duncan, Phillips, M., Roseneil, Sasha, Carter, Julia and Stoilova, Mariya. "Living apart together: uncoupling intimacy and co-residence." *The Sociology Teacher*. 3. (2013). https://www.academia.edu/4137288/Living _Apart_Together_uncoupling_intimacy_and_co_residence

203. Bowman, *Living Apart Together: Legal Protections for a New Form of Family*, 145.

204. Ibid, 152.

205. Colin Perkel, "Unmarried Ontario couple had no children and no house but man must still pay support, appeal court rules," *National Post*, Sept. 10, 2020, accessed Dec. 19, 2022, https://nationalpost.com/news/canada/no-home-or -kids-together-but-couple-still-spouses-appeal-court-rules

206. Christopher Crisman-Cox, "Living apart together relationships," Miller Thomson, May 6, 2021, accessed Dec. 23, 2022, https://www.millerthomson. com/en/blog/family-law-blog/living-apart-together-relationships

207. Simon Duncan, Carter, Julia, Phillips, Miranda, Roseneil, Sasha, and Stoilova, Mariya. "Legal rights for people who 'Live Apart Together'?" *Journal of Social Welfare and Family Law*, 34:4, 4(2012): 443–458, http://dx.doi.org/10.1080 /09649069.2012.753731

208. Vicky Lyssens-Danneboom, Eggermont, Sven, and Mortelmans, Dimitri. "Living Apart Together (LAT) and Law." *Social & Legal Studies* 22, no. 3 (June 7, 2013): 357–76. http://dx.doi.org/10.1177/0964663913478960

209. Diana Adams, phone conversation with author, Nov. 30, 2022.

210. Bowman, *Living Apart Together: Legal Protections for a New Form of Family*, 161.

211. Cynthia Grant Bowman, phone conversation with author, Dec. 7, 2022.

212. Jeffrey M. Jones, "How Many Americans Have a Will?" Gallup, June 23, 2021, accessed Dec. 23, 2022, https://news.gallup.com/poll/351500/how-many -americans-have-will.aspx

213. Bowman, *Living Apart Together: Legal Protections for a New Form of Family*, 47.

214. Lisa Lubin, phone conversation with author, Oct. 21, 2022.

215. Leah Rockwell, "My Partner and I Are 'Living Apart Together' and Our Relationship Is All the Better for It," *Good Housekeeping*, Aug. 25, 2022, accessed Dec. 23, 2022, https://www.goodhousekeeping.com/life/relationships/a40967196/living-apart-together

216. Lauren Apfel, "My girlfriend moved to my city to be closer to me. We decided to live apart for the benefit of our children," *Insider*, Feb. 8, 2022, accessed Dec. 23, 2022, https://www.insider.com/couple-lives-in-separate-homes-benefit-of-their-children-2022-2

217. Kavitha Cardoza, Clare Marie Schneider, "The Key to Stepparenting: Be Patient, It Takes Time," *NPR Lifekit*, Aug. 19, 2021, accessed Dec. 30, 2022, https://www.npr.org/2021/08/16/1028197246/step-parenting-advice-dos-donts-family

218. Livia Sz. Oláh, Karlsson, Lena, and Sandström, Glenn. "Living-Apart-Together (LAT) in Contemporary Sweden: (How) Does It Relate to Vulnerability?" *Journal of Family Issues* 44(1), (2023): 3–24. https://doi.org/10.1177/0192513X211041988

219. Stoessel, *Living Happily Ever After—Separately*, 48.

220. Ibid, 51.

221. Ibid, 44-45.

222. Elif Shafak, "Happily married, 1,500 miles apart," *Red Online*, Feb. 2, 2017, accessed Dec. 20, 2022, https://www.redonline.co.uk/red-women/blogs/a518987/happily-married-1500-miles-apart/

223. Piya Chattopadhyay, host. "'A new way of doing it,' how a divorced couple with children became next door neighbours." *Out in the Open CBC*, Aug. 18, 2017, accessed Nov. 28, 2022, https://www.cbc.ca/radio/outintheopen/conquering-divide-1.4249833/a-new-way-of-doing-it-how-a-divorced-couple-with-children-became-next-door-neighbours-1.4249853

224. Corinne Heller, "Gwyneth Paltrow Talks Co-Parenting With Chris Martin: 'It's Been Hard,'" *E! Online*, July 18, 2015, accessed Dec. 31, 2022, https://www.eonline.com/news/677687/gwyneth-paltrow-talks-co-parenting-with-chris-martin-it-s-been-hard

225. Government of Canada, "High-conflict Separation and Divorce: Options for Consideration," accessed Jan. 13, 2023, https://www.justice.gc.ca/eng/rp-pr/fl-lf/divorce/2004_1/p3.html; Hal Arkowitz, Lilienfeld, Scott O., "Is Divorce Bad for Children?" *Scientific American*, March 1, 2013, accessed Jan. 13, 2023, https://www.scientificamerican.com/article/is-divorce-bad-for-children

226. Susan Golombok. *Modern Families: Parents and Children in New Family Forms.* (Cambridge, U.K., Cambridge University Press, 2015.) doi:10.1017 /CBO9781107295377, page 6

227. Jani Turunen, Fransson, E., and Bergström, M. "Self-esteem in children in joint physical custody and other living arrangements." *Public Health,* 149, (2017): 106–112. https://doi.org/10.1016/j.puhe.2017.04.009

228. Nancy Carlsson-Paige, phone conversation with author, April 21, 2023.

229. Benjamin Butterworth, "Platonic couple who live separately made legal parents of surrogate child," *I News,* March 13, 2018, accessed Jan. 2, 2022, https:// inews.co.uk/news/platonic-couple-who-live-separately-made-legal-parents-of -surrogate-child-134811

230. Claire Gillespie, "What Is Platonic Parenting?" Yahoo The Week, Feb. 17, 2020, accessed May 1, 2023, https://news.yahoo.com/platonic-parenting-105501365. html

231. Deja Thomas, "As family structures change in U.S., a growing share of Americans say it makes no difference," Pew Research Center, April 10, 2020, accessed Dec. 31, 2022, https://www.pewresearch.org/fact-tank/2020/04/10/as-family -structures-change-in-u-s-a-growing-share-of-americans-say-it-makes-no -difference

232. Family by Design, "Talking With Your Younger Child About Your Co-Parenting Relationship," accessed Jan. 2, 2023, http://www.familybydesign.com/content /learn/parenting/talking-with-your-younger-child-about-your-co-parenting -relationship

233. Richard Glotzer, and Cairns Federlein, Anne. "Miles That Bind: Commuter Marriage and Family Strengths." *Michigan Family Review* 12 (2007): 7, http:// dx.doi.org/10.3998/mfr.4919087.0012.102

234. Judith Newman, "For some couples, distance is key to closeness," NBC News, Nov. 4, 2007, accessed March 25, 2023, https://www.nbcnews.com/health /health-news/some-couples-distance-key-closeness-flna1c9464235

235. Harriet Eisenkraft, "Commuter couples who make it work," *University Affairs,* June 11, 2012, accessed Jan. 13, 2023, https://www.universityaffairs. ca/features/feature-article/living-apart-together

236. Danielle J. Lindemann, *Commuter Spouses: New Families in a Changing World* (Ithaca, NY: Cornell University Press, 2019.) http://www.jstor.org /stable/10.7591/j.ctvvndj6, page 53.

237. Hoefle, *Parenting as Partners: How to Launch Your Kids Without Ejecting Your Spouse,* pages 7–8.

238. Vittoria Traverso and Robbins, Jake. "Is 'platonic parenting' the relationship of the future?" BBC Generation Project, Dec.18, 2018, accessed Jan. 2, 2023, https://www.bbc.com/worklife/article/20181218-is-platonic-parenting-the -relationship-of-the-future

239. Abby Ellin, "Making a Child, Minus the Couple," *The New York Times*, Feb. 8, 2013, accessed Jan. 2, 2023. https://www.nytimes.com/2013/02/10/fashion /seeking-to-reproduce-without-a-romantic-partnership.html

240. Shuang Qiu. "Chinese 'Study Mothers' in Living Apart Together (LAT) Relationships: Educational Migration, Family Practices, and Gender Roles." *Sociological Research Online* (2019)., 1360780419871574

241. Fan Yiying and Shiyu, Zhang, "The Chinese Couples Going Dutch on Literally Everything," *Sixth Tone*, Jan. 29, 2021, accessed Jan. 7, 2023, https://www. sixthtone.com/news/1006778/the-chinese-couples-going-dutch-on-literally -everything

242. Debby Herbenick, Rosenberg, Molly, Golzarri-Arroyo, Lilian, Fortenberry, J. Dennis, and Fu, Tsung-chieh. "Changes in Penile-Vaginal Intercourse Frequency and Sexual Repertoire from 2009 to 2018: Findings from the National Survey of Sexual Health and Behavior." *Archives of Sexual Behavior* 51, no. 3 (Nov. 19, 2021): 1419–33. https://doi.org/10.1007/s10508-021-02125-2.

243. Jo Hartley, "5 frankly brilliant benefits of 'living apart together,'" *Body + Soul*, Nov. 10, 2017, accessed Feb. 11, 2023, https://www.bodyandsoul.com. au/mind-body/wellbeing/5-frankly-brilliant-benefits-of-living-apart-together /news-story/8bff102d0ea6f00d8180221c5dd186fc

244. Arman Khan, "For These Committed Couples, Living Apart Is Key to Staying Together," *Vice*, Jan. 17, 2022, accessed Feb. 11, 2023, https://www.vice.com /en/article/wxdgjm/living-apart-together-relationships-marriage-sex

245. Marilisaraccoglobal, "Do couples living apart hold the secret to everlasting love?" *Global News*, July 23, 2018, accessed Feb. 11, 2023, https://globalnews. ca/news/4318749/living-apart-together-couples/

246. Kate Sloan, "The 6 best sex toys for couples in a long-distance relationship," *Insider*, Oct 19, 2022, accessed Feb. 20, 2023. https://www.insider.com/guides /health/sex-relationships/best-bluetooth-sex-toys

247. Gregory Guldner, "Long Distance Relationship Frequently Asked Questions," The Center for the Study of Long Distance Relationships, accessed Feb. 20, 2023, https://www.longdistancerelationships.net/faqs.htm

248. Bianca Mendez, "6 Ways to Keep the Sexual Sparks Flying in a Long-Distance Relationship," *Greatist*, May 14, 2019, accessed Feb. 20, 2023, https://greatist.

com/live/long-distance-sex

249. Fran Lu, "'Where's the tongue?': creepy Chinese kissing contraption offers long-distance, lip-smacking 'real-life' encounters of the smooching kind," *South China Morning Post*, Feb. 24, 2023, accessed March 9, 2023, https://www.scmp.com/news/people-culture/trending-china/article/3211089/wheres-tongue-creepy-chinese-kissing-contraption-offers-long-distance-lip-smacking-real-life

250. Eric Marlowe Garrison, phone conversation with author, May 22, 2023.

251. Alexandra-Andreea Ciritel, "Sexual intimacy and relationship happiness in living apart together, cohabiting, and married relationships: evidence from Britain," *Genus* 78, 32 (2022). https://doi.org/10.1186/s41118-022-00178-2

252. Sasha Roseneil. "On not living with a partner: Unpicking coupledom and cohabitation." *Sociological Research Online*, 11(3), (2006): 111–124.

253. Alexandra-Andreea Ciritel. "Does Sex Matter? The Role of Sexual and Relationship Satisfaction on Living Apart Together Relationship Transitions." *Comparative Population Studies* 47 (December 2022). Wiesbaden, Germany. https://doi.org/10.12765/CPoS-2022-18

254. Jacquelyn Benson, Kerr, Steffany, and Ermer, Ashley. "Living apart together relationships in later life: Constructing an account of relational maintenance." *Contemporary Perspectives in Family Research*, 11, (2017): 193–215. https://doi.org/10.1108/S1530-353520170000011009

255. Sandra L. Murray, et al. "Tempting fate or inviting happiness?: Unrealistic idealization prevents the decline of marital satisfaction." *Psychological Science* vol. 22, 5 (2011): 619–26. doi:10.1177/0956797611403155

256. Annie Fox, "Can Everyone Please Stop Freaking Out That My Husband and I Don't Live Together," *Glamour*, Sept. 7, 2016, accessed March 25, 2023, https://www.glamour.com/story/can-everyone-please-stop-freaking-out-that-my-husband-and-i-dont-live-together

257. Jenny de Jong Gierveld. "Intra-couple caregiving of older adults living apart together: Commitment and independence." *Canadian Journal on Aging = La Revue Canadienne du Vieillissement*, 34 (Special Issue 3), (2015): 356–365. https://doi.org/10.1017/S0714980815000264

258 University of Missouri News Release, "Are Couples Who Choose To Live Apart Tested When Partners Require Caregiving," Jan. 8, 2018, accessed March 9, 2023, https://munewsarchives.missouri.edu/news-releases/2018/0108-are-couples-who-choose-to-live-apart-tested-when-partners-require-caregiving

259. Judith Newman, "He's Going Back to His Former Wife. Sort Of," *The New*

York Times, June 29, 2018, accessed March 25, 2023, https://www.nytimes.com/2018/06/29/style/modern-love-hes-going-back-to-his-former-wife-sort-of.html

260. University of Missouri News Release, "Older Adults Embracing 'Living Apart Together,'" Feb. 9, 2017, accessed March 9, 2023, https://munewsarchives.missouri.edu/news-releases/2017/0209-older-adults-embracing-living-apart-together

261. Vicki Larson, "Never too late to find love, says Mill Valley's Eve Pell," *Marin Independent Journal*, Jan. 26, 2015, accessed March 11, 2023, https://www.marinij.com/2015/01/26/never-too-late-to-find-love-says-mill-valleys-eve-pell/

262. Wednesday Martin, "Guess Who Has the Power in a Remarriage with Children?" *Psychology Today*, Oct. 7, 2009, accessed March 11, 2023, https://www.psychologytoday.com/us/blog/stepmonster/200910/guess-who-has-the-power-in-a-remarriage-children

263. Linda Bernstein, "What to Do When Your Adult Kids Hate That You're in Love Again," *Next Avenue*, Feb. 11, 2013, accessed March 11, 2023, https://www.nextavenue.org/what-do-when-your-adult-kids-hate-youre-love-again

264. Judith Graham, "Living Apart Together: A New Option for Older Adults," Kaiser Health News, May 11, 2018, accessed March 9, 2023, https://khn.org/news/living-apart-together-a-new-option-for-older-adults/

265. Francine Russo, "Older Singles Have Found a New Way to Partner Up: Living Apart," *The New York Times*, July 16, 2021, accessed Oct. 1, 2022, https://www.nytimes.com/2021/07/16/well/family/older-singles-living-apart-LAT.html

266. Nytasia Hicks. "'It's a care free way of life': A qualitative descriptive study on living-apart-together relationships among older black women." Doctoral dissertation, Miami University, 2020. http://rave.ohiolink.edu/etdc/view?acc_num=miami1595603122018959

267. Dee Cascio, phone conversation with author, April 3, 2023.

268. McMaster University, "Making the transition to retirement," McMaster Optimal Aging Portal, April 24, 2019, accessed March 17, 2023, https://www.mcmasteroptimalaging.org/blog/detail/blog/2019/04/24/making-the-transition-to-retirement

269. Pierre Cachia. "Supporting Links Between Living Apart Together (LAT) Couples Through Online Couple Therapy" In: Abela, A., Vella, S., Piscopo, S. (eds) *Couple Relationships in a Global Context*. European Family Therapy Association Series. (2020). Springer, Cham, page 381, https://doi.org/10.1007/978-3

-030-37712-0_23

270. Pierre Cachia, phone conversation with author, March 17, 2023.

271. Chaya Koren and Ayalon, Liat. "Not living together yet all the time together: The construction of living apart together in continuing care retirement communities from perspectives of residents and CCRC staff," *Journal of Social and Personal Relationships* 36.11-12 (2019): 3855–3874, https://doi.org/10.1177/0265407519840; Chaya Koren and Ayalon, Liat. "Envy and Jealousy of Living-Apart-Together Relationships in Continuing Care Retirement Communities." *Innovation in Aging* 4 (Suppl 1), (2020), 382. https://doi.org/10.1093/geroni/igaa057.1231

272. Catherine Hawes, Phillips, C. D., Rose, M., Holan, S., and Sherman, M. "High service or high privacy assisted living facilities, their residents and staff: results from a national survey," U.S. Department of Health and Human Services, Office of Disability, Aging and Long-Term Care Policy, (2000), https://aspe.hhs.gov/reports/high-service-or-high-privacy-assisted-living-facilities-their-residents-staff-results-national-1#chap3

273. Chaya Koren and Ayalon, Liat. "Not living together yet all the time together: The construction of living apart together in continuing care retirement communities from perspectives of residents and CCRC staff," *Journal of Social and Personal Relationships* 36.11-12 (2019): 3855–3874, https://doi.org/10.1177/0265407519840

274. Ayanna Alexander, "LGBTQ Elders Fear Being Shoved in Closet in Nursing Care Hunt," *Bloomberg Law*, June 28, 2022, accessed March 20, 2023, https://news.bloomberglaw.com/social-justice/gay-elders-fear-being-shoved-back-in-closet-in-nursing-care-hunt

275. Caterina Trevisan, Grande, G., Vetrano, D. L., Maggi, S., Sergi, G., Welmer, A. K., and Rizzuto, D. "Gender Differences in the Relationship Between Marital Status and the Development of Frailty: A Swedish Longitudinal Population-Based Study." *Journal of Women's Health* (2002), 29(7), (2020): 927–936 10.1089/jwh.2019.8095; Caterina Trevisan, Veronese, N., Maggi, S., Baggio, G., De Rui, M., Bolzetta, F., Zambon, S., Sartori, L., Perissinotto, E., Crepaldi, G., Manzato, E., and Sergi, G. "Marital Status and Frailty in Older People: Gender Differences in the Progetto Veneto Anziani Longitudinal Study." *Journal of Women's Health* (2002), 25(6), (2016): 630–637. https://doi.org/10.1089/jwh.2015.5592

276. Marti Benedetti and Dempsey, Mary A., *Finding Love After Loss: A Relationship Roadmap for Widows* (Lanham, Md.: Rowman & Littlefield, October 2021).

277. E. A. Marconi, emails with author, Aug. 6, 2022, March 11, 2023.

278. Celia Walden, "I took a six-week marriage sabbatical—and it worked wonders." *The Telegraph*, Aug. 16, 2022, accessed Oct. 30, 2022, https://www.telegraph. co.uk/columnists/2022/08/16/took-six-week-marriage-sabbatical-worked-wonders/

279. Bettijane Levine, "After Pause, a Couple Reconcile Their Aims," *Los Angeles Times*, April 30, 2002, accessed Oct. 30, 2022, https://www.latimes.com /archives/la-xpm-2002-apr-30-lv-runaway30-story.html

280. Ruby Warrington, "How a woman took an eight month marriage SABBAT-ICAL and went alone to Ibiza. Now her husband agrees, it saved them from divorce." *Daily Mail*, April 9, 2017, accessed Oct. 30, 2022, https://www. dailymail.co.uk/femail/article-4395896/Couple-say-marriage-sabbatical-saved -divorce.html

281. Leigh Shulman, "My husband and I don't live together anymore. It's improved our marriage." *Insider*, Oct. 22, 2022, accessed Oct. 30, 2022, https:// www.insider.com/married-couple-doesnt-live-together-anymore-it-improved -relationship-2022-10

282. Lindsay Tigar, "4 Couples Who Went to the Extreme to Save Their Marriage." *Redbook*, Jan. 16, 2015, accessed Oct. 1, 2022, https://www.redbookmag. com/love-sex/news/a19836/4-couples-who-went-to-the-extreme-to-save-their -marriage/?click=_lpTrnsprtr_1

283. Stoessel, *Living Happily Ever After—Separately*, page 31.

284. Kelly Coyne, "The Wife Left, but They're Still Together," *The New York Times*, Dec. 10, 2022, accessed Dec. 11, 2022, https://www.nytimes.com/2022/12/10 /style/living-apart-together-marriage.html

285. Crystal Hammon, "Separate Homes Help Heal Troubled Marriage," *Next Avenue*, Aug. 15, 2019, accessed Dec. 16, 2022, https://www.nextavenue.org separate-homes-help-heal-troubled-marriage

286. Maria Noyen, "A married couple spent 8 months living separately to save the relationship—then moved back in together," *Insider*, Aug. 6, 2022, accessed Oct. 30, 2022, https://www.insider.com/couple-spent-8-months-living -separately-would-do-it-again-2022-8

287. Sana Akhand, Instagram, Nov. 8, 2022, accessed Dec. 12, 2022, https://www. instagram.com/p/Ckt97AJvCF5/?utm_source=ig_web_copy_link

288. Rebecca Huff, "When and How to Write Your Own Healing Separation Agree-ment," *That Organic Mom*, March 10, 2021, accessed Dec. 16, 2022, https:// www.thatorganicmom.com/healing-separation-agreement

289. Rebecca Huff, "Pros and Cons of Living Apart Together While Married," *That Organic Mom*, March 10, 2021, accessed Dec. 16, 2022, https://www.thatorganicmom.com/living-apart-together/

290. Stephanie Foo, host, "Home. Alone," *Home. Made* (podcast), Sept. 1, 2023, accessed Oct. 30, 2023 https://www.rocketmortgage.com/learn/podcast-episode-5

291. Tim Lott, "Why living apart together is worth a try," *The Guardian*, Nov. 24, 2017, accessed Dec. 16, 2022, https://www.theguardian.com/lifeandstyle/2017/nov/24/i-tried-living-apart-from-my-wife-to-save-our-marriage

292 Susan Pease Gadoua, "Can a Temporary Separation Make a Relationship Stronger?" *Psychology Today*, April 25, 2010, accessed Dec. 16, 2022, https://www.psychologytoday.com/us/blog/contemplating-divorce/201004/can-temporary-separation-make-relationship-stronger

293. Ronnie Koenig and Ree Hines, "Carson Daly says he and wife Siri don't always sleep together: 'It's the best thing,'" *Today*, June 14, 2020, accessed March 31, 2023, https://www.today.com/popculture/carson-daly-wife-siri-say-they-ll-continue-their-sleep-t184252

294. Jennifer Adams. *Sleeping Apart Not Falling Apart: How to Get a Good Night's Sleep and Keep Your Relationship Alive* (Chicago, Illinois Publishing, 2015), page ix.

295. Stephanie J. Wilson, Jaremka, Lisa M., Fagundes, Christopher P., Andridge, Rebecca, Peng, Juan, Malarkey, William B., Habash, Diane, Belury, Martha A., and Kiecolt-Glaser, Janice K. "Shortened sleep fuels inflammatory responses to marital conflict: Emotion regulation matters." *Psychoneuroendocrinology* 79, (2017): 74–83. https://doi.org/10.1016/j.psyneuen.2017.02.015

296. Ganda Suthivarakom, "Share a Bed Without Losing Sleep," *The New York Times*, March 18, 2019, accessed March 31, 2023, https://www.nytimes.com/2019/03/18/smarter-living/wirecutter/how-to-share-bed-sleep-partner.html

297. Wendy M. Troxel, TEDx talk, "How to Sleep Like Your Relationship Depends on It," Jan. 27, 2020, accessed March 31, 2023, https://youtu.be/U7ntoFtZK6A

298. Devon Haynie, "Countries Where the Most Young Adults Live With Their Parents," *U.S. News & World Report*, Oct. 5, 2016, accessed April 23, 2023, https://www.usnews.com/news/best-countries/articles/2016-10-05/countries-where-the-most-young-adults-live-with-their-parents

299. Richard Fry, Passel, Jeffrey S., and Cohn, D'Vera. "A majority of young adults in the U.S. live with their parents for the first time since the Great Depression,"

Pew Research Center, Sept. 4, 2020, accessed April 23, 2023, https://www.pewresearch.org/short-reads/2020/09/04/a-majority-of-young-adults-in-the-u-s-live-with-their-parents-for-the-first-time-since-the-great-depression

300. Erica Pandey, "America the Single," *Axios*, Feb. 25, 2023, accessed Feb. 27, 2023, https://www.axios.com/2023/02/25/marriage-declining-single-dating-taxes-relationships; Esteban Ortiz-Ospina and Roser, Max, "Marriages and Divorces." OurWorldInData.org (2020), https://ourworldindata.org/marriages-and-divorces

301. Esteban Ortiz-Ospina and Roser, Max, "Marriages and Divorces." OurWorldInData.org (2020), https://ourworldindata.org/marriages-and-divorces

302. Harry Enten, "Americans less likely to have sex, partner up and get married than ever," CNN, Feb. 14, 2022, accessed Feb. 27, 2023, https://www.cnn.com/2022/02/14/health/valentines-day-love-marriage-relationships-wellness/index.html

303. James M. Raymo, Park, H., Xie, Y., and Yeung, W. J. "Marriage and Family in East Asia: Continuity and Change." *Annual Review of Sociology*, 41 (2015), 471–492. https://doi.org/10.1146/annurev-soc-073014-112428

304 Veronica L. Gregorio, "Living Apart Together: Debates, Variations, and Research Opportunities." *Philippine Sociological Review*, Vol. 68 (2020), pp. 55–74.

305. Laura Carlson, Sz. Oláh, Livia, and Hobson, Barbara, "Policy recommendations: Changing families and sustainable societies: Policy contexts and diversity over the life course and across generations," FamiliesAndSocieties, 2017, accessed May 13, 2023, http://www.familiesandsocieties.eu/wp-content/uploads/2017/06/WorkingPaper78.pdf

306. Jessica Guynn, "Netflix is cracking down on password sharing. How about HBO Max, Disney+, Hulu and others?" *USA Today*, Feb. 14, 2023, accessed April 15, 2023, https://www.usatoday.com/story/money/2023/02/14/netflix-disney-hulu-password-sharing/11222904002

307. Erick Trickey, "How Minneapolis Freed Itself From the Stranglehold of Single-Family Homes," Politico Magazine, July 11, 2019, accessed April 24, 2023, https://www.politico.com/magazine/story/2019/07/11/housing-crisis-single-family-homes-policy-227265/;

308. Christian Britschgi, "Oregon Becomes First State to Ditch Single-Family Zoning," *Reason*, July, 1, 2019, accessed April 24, 2023, https://reason.com/2019/07/01/oregon-becomes-first-state-to-ditch-single-family-zoning/

309. Manuela Tobias, "California's housing crisis: How much difference will a

new zoning law make?" *Cal Matters*, Aug. 19, 2021, accessed April 24, 2023, https://calmatters.org/housing/2021/08/california-housing-crisis-zoning-bill/

310. Karen Chum, Fitzhenry, G., Robinson, K., Murphy, M., Phan, D., Alvarez, J., Hand, C., Laliberte Rudman, D., McGrath, C., "Examining community-based housing models to support aging in place: A scoping review," *The Gerontologist* vol. 62,3 (2022): e178-e192. doi:10.1093/geront/gnaa142

311. Kathleen E. Hull, Meier, A., and Ortyl, T. "The Changing Landscape of Love and Marriage." *Contexts* (Berkeley, Calif.), 9(2), (2010): 32–37. https://doi.org/10.1525/ctx.2010.9.2.32

312. Website retired, accessed April 10, 2023, https://www.rewire.org/living-apart-together

313. Lynn Jamieson, "Between the couple and living alone" in Abela, A., Vella, S., and Piscopo, S. (eds,), *Couple Relationships in a Global Context: Understanding Love and Intimacy Across Cultures.* European Family Therapy Association Series, 2020, Springer, Cham, pp. 329–344. https://doi.org/10.1007/978-3-030-37712-0_20

314. Arnaud Regnier-Loilier, Beaujouan, Éva, and Villeneuve-Gokalp, Catherine. "Neither Single, nor in a Couple. A Study of Living Apart Together in France." *Demographic Research* 21 (2009), pages 75–87. https://doi.org/10.4054/demres.2009.21.4.

315. Rhaina Cohen, "What If Friendship, Not Marriage, Was at the Center of Life?" *The Atlantic*, Oct. 20, 2020, accessed April 15, 2023, https://www.theatlantic.com/family/archive/2020/10/people-who-prioritize-friendship-over-romance/616779

316. Mariya Stoilova, Roseneil, Sasha, Carter, Julia, Duncan, Simon, and Phillips, Miranda. "Constructions, reconstructions and deconstructions of 'family' amongst people who live apart together (LATs)." *The British Journal of Sociology* 68. (2016). 10.1111/1468-4446.12220.

ACKNOWLEDGEMENTS

I started writing about live apart relationships more than a decade ago, but I have been living as one with various romantic partners for twice as long. I have experienced the questions, judgments, and dismissive comments of others—and sometimes their envy—as well as my own ambivalence about it at times. Anytime you choose to have a romantic relationship that's outside the norm, it can be confusing. And so, I have tried to capture in this book the many ways the LAT lifestyle can be joyous and challenging at the same time.

A book about LATs couldn't be written without the many academics who have studied it, both in the United States and abroad, and whose research greatly informs this book. While studies matter, the stories from people who have chosen to live apart from their romantic partner are just as important—they're the ones who have figured out what it takes day after day to stay connected while separate. Their stories liven and enrich this book, and I thank them for generously sharing their lives with me, honestly addressing what's worked and what hasn't, and what they would like others to know.

I am also profoundly grateful for the many experts who offered their thoughtful advice on dealing with some of the potential pitfalls LAT couples may face.

Of course, this book would not have happened if it hadn't caught the eye of the editors at Cleis Press, who believed, as I do, that a book like this needed to be written. I thank them for having faith that I was the one to do it. And I thank my editor, Ashley Calvano, and copy editor, Sara Brady, for making my manuscript shine. Finally, I thank my wonderful sons, Nash and Kit, who showed me that children can thrive even if their parents don't live together, E. C., who generously helped me find a concept for the book's cover that wasn't heteronormative, gendered, or cliché, and my dear friends the Lovelies, who have long listened with open hearts and minds to my outside-the-box relationship ideas, and who keep me grounded, honest, humble, and always laughing.